W9-AJO-177

ANSWERS

ANSWERS

A Divine Connection

Yvonne M. Albanese

HAMPTON ROADS
PUBLISHING COMPANY, INC.

Copyright © 2000
by Yvonne M. Albanese

All rights reserved, including the right to reproduce this
work in any form whatsoever, without permission
in writing from the publisher, except for brief passages
in connection with a review.

Cover design by Marjoram Productions
Cover art by Louis Jones
The poem *Footprints* used with permission

For information write:

Hampton Roads Publishing Company, Inc.
1125 Stoney Ridge Road
Charlottesville, VA 22902

Or call: 804-296-2772
FAX: 804-296-5096
e-mail: hrpc@hrpub.com
Web site: www.hrpub.com

If you are unable to order this book from your local
bookseller, you may order directly from the publisher.
Call 1-800-766-8009, toll-free.

Library of Congress Catalog Card Number: 00-105252

ISBN 1-57174-192-5
10 9 8 7 6 5 4 3 2 1

Printed on acid-free paper in Canada

For all those who are searching
for their own answers

Acknowledgments

I would like to express my gratitude to all who have helped me on my spiritual path. It has been a long journey and I still have far to go. My family is an integral part of this journey. I have never strayed far from those I love. I would not be able to live without them—those on Earth and those in Heaven. Thank you to all! Thank you also to my dear husband Giacomo, my son Jake, and my daughter Marianna—the three dearest, most precious people in my life. They provided the inspiration for many of my questions. Most of all, thank you, dear God, for the wondrous blessing of your communication with me. I sincerely hope that I am able to inspire others with my experience.

Foreword

It is such an honor and great pleasure to write the Foreword of this book. *Answers: A Divine Connection* came into my life when I was questioning my own journey and how God fit into the scheme of things for me.

Let me start by telling you a little about myself and how I came to meet the extraordinary Yvonne Albanese. I have been a practicing spiritualist for the past ten years. Being guided by spirit is the very crux of my craft. Hence, I know that God has always been the major force in my calling. I have no doubt that the messages I receive emanate from the Lord. By what route and to what extent was still somewhat of a mystery to me until I read *Answers*.

We all go through life with the hope that God will speak to us. He does. He speaks to every one of us; all we have to do is ask for his guidance and he will be there to assist us through our hardships. We "know" this, yet we seek tangible proof that he does indeed exist. God speaks to my clients through me in my readings, for my readings come from the purest of hearts. They are honest and accurate and they provide the kind of warmth to my clients that I know I would have a difficult time expressing if not for the Lord guiding me through it.

I see a lot of things in my readings. I see sadness, pain, suffering, frustration, loneliness, grief; but most of all, I see that people are desperately trying to feel a part of something—something bigger than what they now have. They need to feel God's love and need to hear his words of encouragement. I see their sadness and confusion transformed into a better understanding of why they experience what they do; an outcome can always be forecast that makes them feel, ultimately, prosperous, spiritually fulfilled and connected. I do this well because I do it with God's guidance, always.

Oftentimes, my clients will ask me questions about God—and what he has in store for them, and if their loved ones who have passed on are with God. They ask me if an afterlife really exists. They ask many more, deeply profound, questions, which I've always answered to the best of my knowledge. But I was limited as to what I could answer, until I read the words of Yvonne Albanese's book—the most inspiring I have ever read.

I am convinced that God uses me as one of his messengers, and for that I am so grateful. But be that as it may, sometimes I get overwhelmed by all the suffering I see in my clients' lives, as well as that of my own. I've been moved to ask similar questions, like: Why is there suffering? Why is there greed? Why is there violence? Why is there prejudice in the world? Where does it all come from? It is the very God-given gift of my calling that continually exposes me to these heart-wrenching questions; and they've weighed very heavily on my mind and in my heart.

I went through a difficult period of time, seemingly never having enough hours in a day to accomplish what I was supposed to do. All too often, time escaped me. By nightfall, I was weary, utterly exhausted—so much so that I became remiss in my favorite pastime, reading. I am what you'd call an avid reader. One look into the contents of my bookcases will attest to that. The day my friend Irene handed me a copy of *Answers* to read, I was hooked. Yvonne's spiritual essence leapt from the pages that I was devouring. I could not put this book down. I couldn't help feeling that this book was written just for me. All the questions I'd had pertaining to God's ultimate plan were laid out right before my eyes. The answers to the deep questions posed by my clients, family, and friends were spelled out for us all to know and share.

Yvonne Albanese communicates her questions and thoughts to God in a way that is heartfelt and inspiring. I wept out loud as I read it. Her words brought me to tears, again and again. I finished reading *Answers* within four hours. It left me with a feeling of peace and a deep innner knowing that God does, indeed, answer all of our questions. My confidence was bolstered and I was enabled to guide clients and loved ones in a more profound way than I could have before reading it. It gave me hope—something we all need an extra dose of at times in our lives.

When I finally met Yvonne Albanese, let me tell you, the experience was just as powerful as that of reading her book. Yvonne had made an appointment with me for a psychic reading and to learn a little about what I saw in her future. I made the appointment never realizing it was the Yvonne who had written the book that I was utterly enchanted by. When Yvonne sat down across from me, I immediately felt that same calming and tranquil feeling that I get when I "experience" her book. I read for Yvonne that night, telling her that she was gifted and creative and that she had a bright future ahead of her. I gave her time frames within which to expect events to take place that were going to open up for her, as well as when things in her life were going to close. All this time, I was still unaware that I was reading for the author of the book that so positively changed my life.

At the end of the reading, Yvonne said that she was amazed by my accuracy, and she asked me if I was able to pick up what it is that she does for a living. I told her that I wasn't receiving her profession per se, but I knew that it was her own and that she was using her creative abilities to achieve it. She then told me she had written a book. Both Yvonne and her book evoked a flood of emotion in me, an emotional release that had been building for a long time. Emotion that only the will of God can produce. I knew by her words and the spirit of her essence that God does indeed exist.

I was in the company of one blessed by the voice of God. I felt joy in my heart and a spring in my step as I rushed to herald the news that God does answer our questions regarding good versus evil. Why there is crime and why there is abandonment. Each answered question leaves the reader with a sense of peace and the feeling that they themselves have been touched by God. In my opinion, anyone who reads this book will certainly feel most lovingly touched by God.

Some who have not read the book have asked me, "Do you believe that she actually spoke to God?" My response to that is a resounding *yes!* For no person here on Earth can write with such emotion and love and not be touched by God. God is love, and this book is of the purest, deepest love—from cover to cover.

Yvonne Albanese believes and projects through her words that she is just an ordinary woman. But how can that be, when she has created a journey that transforms the unanswered quest of the multitudes of ordinary people into the comfort of answers, by letting us share in her communion with God, which is hardly ordinary.

I am blessed to know, and to have been influenced by, Yvonne Albanese, an ordinary woman with an extraordinary story to share. A story I'll never forget. It is a connection I'll always hold dear.

As you read this book, you'll experience what is intended for all of us to share: the knowledge that God is here. God is love. God does answer our prayers. And God is always with us. God . . . is with you.

Debra Leslie
Spiritualist

Introduction

I feel that it is important to explain how these messages came to me. Since I was a young girl, I have been fascinated with psychic development. I had the ability to occasionally read minds when I was very young, between three and five years of age. I would astound my dear mother with my perceptions. Throughout the course of my life, I realized the importance of this gift, though I had absolutely no control over it. Or so I thought—it is actually within my control, as I am coming to realize. Everyone has this ability and everyone experiences it in fleeting moments. I am not special in this regard. I found that when these experiences took place, I felt wonderful and unbelievably energized for days afterward. I began to explore the communication of departed loved ones who touched my life. I had numerous experiences of communication with people whom I have loved and lost. Every time one of these experiences occurred I felt truly blessed and at peace. I wished that they could occur more frequently—I still have not figured out how to make this happen, but I do believe that it is within my grasp.

I began with trying to communicate with my deceased mother-in-law, Marianna, through automatic writing. To briefly explain what this means, automatic writing is a form of spiritual communication in which you make direct contact with spirit through your writing. Very often the handwriting is not even your own, it takes on the character of whomever you are "speaking" with. It was difficult to receive messages from Marianna. Once in a while I would get a clear phrase, or a sentence or two, and I was very happy to have received it. But I must say I was discouraged. I had truly hoped for more. When I am attempting to perform automatic writing with my mother-in-law, I am not aware of what I am writing. The thoughts don't enter my mind clearly as I write them down. I don't really know what I am getting until later when I read it.

One night at the end of April in 1998, I awoke and could not fall back to sleep no matter how I tried. I got up and made a cup of tea. As I sat at my kitchen table I felt the urge to write, to try to have a communication—I assumed with Marianna. As usual, when I wrote the message, I was not aware of what I was receiving. When I looked down to read it, I saw in red scribble scrabble, but clearly decipherable handwriting: "My child, you are seeking answers to questions. Seek not, for you shall find the answers through me. For I am your God." The moment I finished reading it, I heard my husband calling me. I went back to bed and fell into a deep sleep instantly.

I have to admit that this message I received did not affect me profoundly at first. I did not realize its importance or validity. "Yeah right—God is going to talk to me!" I soon came to realize that was exactly what was going to happen. Days later I awoke again and could not sleep. A question came to my mind. I got up and sat at the kitchen table and received an answer that was beautiful and inspiring. It truly touched me. When I received this message the thoughts entered my mind very loudly and clearly. I wrote as fast as I could, trying to keep up. It was very rapid thinking and it was not my own. I felt like a court stenographer recording a conversation. I was merely transcribing a message that came through my mind. This was pretty amazing!

I have since been receiving answers to questions I ask God on a regular basis. I usually have the greatest success at doing this if I awaken in the wee hours of the night, when my busy household is quiet. When these messages are received, my energy level is very high and a great feeling of love fills me. The room even seems brighter and colors much prettier. I began writing these messages directly into my computer, which was much more comfortable for me. I can type much faster than I can write. I seem to get a lengthier message when I use this approach. So, very often I sit at my computer at three or four in the morning, asking God questions on the most profound subjects.

The messages I receive are my own truth. I have come to find out through God that all truths (beliefs) are significant and are real for each individual. My truth may not be yours. All beliefs lead to God and the pure love that this great force is made up of. How you tap into that source is not important. If you follow a particular religion, that is your truth and it brings you God's messages of love through that particular discipline. All religions are important and every one of them is truth.

I was not sure what to do with these messages when I began writing. Early on, I gave them to my family; all were touched in different ways, some much more profoundly than others. But they told me this is important, maybe the most important thing I ever do in my life. This message is meant to be spread and enjoyed by other like souls on the same path of awakening as I. Through this book I am sharing it with you. If the answers I have provided give inspiration or a further understanding of something you already believed in, that is my mission. I hope it provides light and love to your experience in this life.

Love to all,

Yvonne

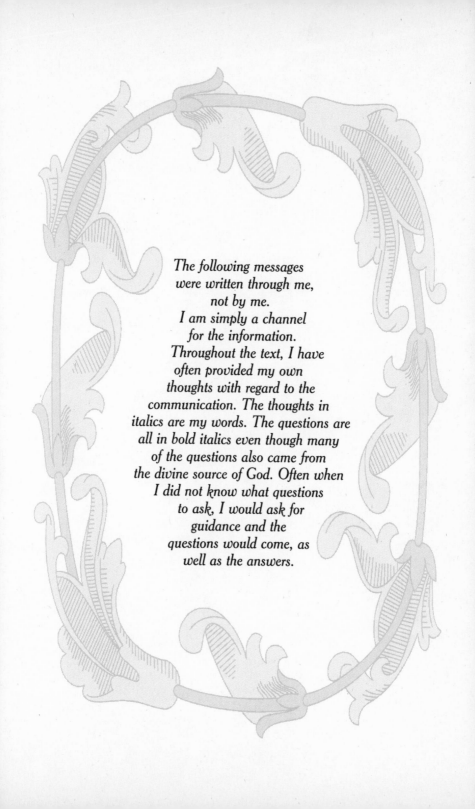

*The following messages
were written through me,
not by me.
I am simply a channel
for the information.
Throughout the text, I have
often provided my own
thoughts with regard to the
communication. The thoughts in
italics are my words. The questions are
all in bold italics even though many
of the questions also came from
the divine source of God. Often when
I did not know what questions
to ask, I would ask for
guidance and the
questions would come, as
well as the answers.*

First Message

My child, you are seeking answers to questions. Seek not, for you shall find the answers through me. For I am your God.

How are souls created?

This great force you call "God" peered into an enormous mirror, not a conventional mirror, but one so beautiful, multi-dimensional, so bright and shining that one would be blinded by its power—totally beyond comprehension or imagination. When I looked into this mirror I could see myself in all my glory—the good, the bad, and all the billions of variations within. And in wanting to experience all of these attributes, I smashed this great, beautiful mirror and sent the glorious, beautiful pieces of myself to the physical world so they could experience life. So that I could thus experience myself in terms of physical time and space. Now, all of these pieces did not necessarily get sent forth to the Earth, but floated freely in space, near me, as if being pulled by gravity towards me. Your time here on the earth plane is limited. You will always be pulled back to the great force you call "God." When that time is, when you come back to me, is completely within your own control. You choose it. You do not consciously realize this.

When you go back (die, so to speak) it is because you choose to do so. Sometimes you have a plan, before you are born into this world, of exactly when that time will be. Often because your experience on the earth plane is so joyful/ intense/delicious, your soul changes its mind and wants to linger, sometimes months, sometimes years. Again, the choice is yours. You do form bonds with other like souls, or souls that you feel you can help along the way on their soul-path evolution. You meet these souls coming and going on Earth and in Heaven, and you are joyful at seeing them again and again. When someone on Earth feels familiar, comfortable, or likable instantly, it's probably because you have been in that soul's presence many times before. In conclusion, you are all pieces of God—beautiful, wonderful pieces encompassing every characterization of what God can be. Good, evil—everything there is.

These mirror pieces that you are, are not inferior versions of God but only of God's image. I have the ultimate power to create new "mirrors" or to change old ones, whatsoever as I choose. It is great fun for me to experience life as you know it here on Earth, and every time you come back and incarnate into a new body and a new life, you get closer to knowing and understanding the wonder of my true essence. Now sleep, my dear child, for I will talk to you again and again.

This first answered question left me with such a wonderful feeling of joy. The way it occurred was so strange. I awoke at about three-fifteen in the morning with the question deeply embedded in my thought: How are souls created? Words started rapidly entering my mind—a reply to this question. I thought to myself, "Stop! I have to get up and write this down!" I literally jumped out of bed (quietly, so as to not wake my husband) and I went downstairs searching for paper and pen. I was so afraid that the answer would be clouded by my own thought process that I kept repeating the question over and over again in my head until I was ready to write down the answer.

When I was finally ready, I asked the question once again. I wrote so rapidly I could barely keep up. I was amazed! I knew that I do not think this fast. When finished, I read what you just read on the previous pages. I found it a very beautiful representation of how God creates souls. I sensed that I should not take it literally, because God was providing the answer through my words. When mere words are used as instruments for understanding, the understanding is limited. Nonetheless, I found these words to be beautiful and inspiring.

I was intrigued. Was this just an overactive imagination? After this message, I did not experience any profound communication with God again for some time. I talk to God just about every day. This is normal for me. I have been talking to God daily for many, many years. However, the written message made me feel so wonderful. I was "high" for a few days. I asked God, "Please, dear God, may I experience this once again?" Soon after, I awoke at just about the same time, a little after three A.M., with a new question.

How can I live the life I want to lead?

Have patience, my child, for everything you ask for, you shall receive, if it is truly what you want to create for yourself. Be positive about it. Do not push it away from you. Think of it as already existing, and it will manifest itself right before your very eyes. Create the life you wish to have. This is your life. Live it to its fullest, to your heart's desire. The desires of the heart are my grandest wish for you. Live by the desires of your heart, and the rest will surely follow. Let go of all that you fear. Love and fear are all that there is. Choose love at every moment in your life, and the fear will melt away and be forever gone.

This is not an easy thing for you to do, but make a concentrated effort to connect with the source you call "God," and love will surely flow into every cell of your being. If you are filled with this love-energy, all adversity will cease to exist. This message is for the entire world. If each human lived a life of love, all strife would disappear, cease to exist. It is the fear in your heart that creates your unhappiness. Be still and concentrate, connect to that "source" and tap into it. The love is enormous and ever-flowing. Use it. Be it. It will bring you great joy.

Is Jesus your son?

Jesus is my son, but not my only son. You are all my children, and my love for you is everlasting and completely non-judgmental. I choose not a single individual to love more or less. The criminal and the saint are all loved the same by me. They are all part of me. I experience my existence through their actions—the good, the bad, everything. My greatest joy is living on Earth through each and every one of you. Jesus was the first human soul to live a life completely of love, with no fear whatsoever. He reached a state of perfect love—one that very few people have been able to achieve in so few lifetimes. You all could live that life, but you are just not ready for it.

There is a progression, of sorts. Often a few steps forward and then a few steps back. But don't despair. Enjoy the wonderful roller-coaster ride. Embrace that love and try to live it. You will then be moving toward Christness of being. You can choose whatsoever you wish. The joy is in the journey, not the journey's end.

Even Christ, who reached absolute perfection, will choose to return to the earth plane because life is so wonderful to experience—the struggles, the pain, the unlimited joy of experience and learning and change, of history, of evolution. It is all desirable to the souls of many. Very few souls choose to remain in "Heaven" forever. They just can't help themselves—they want to return again and again. It's like going on a vacation to a wonderful and exciting place, where you can experience anything imaginable and everything imaginable. But just like going on a vacation, you wish to return home to me; for this Heaven you speak of is your home. And it is to home that you shall always return. Your return is with great joy and familiarity. You love being home.

Only love exists in this place called "home." But you can't help yourself—that vacation on Earth calls to you, and you long to experience life again on the earth plane. All of it you love. You carefully choose your destination, planning where you want to go and with whom. When you are born into this new life, it is not at all by chance. It is of your own choosing. Your parents are your choice. So love them, imperfections and all. Live with your choice, because that is what *you* chose to experience.

When you are on Earth your original plan is forgotten by your conscious mind-being, but it's in there and your subconscious knows what it is. Try to remember it, for your original plan will take you to a higher level of being that will bring you much happiness. Just like a vacation, your original plans often change. That is okay. That is your human mind and body's free will, and it will always have free will over the soul on the earth plane. That is part of the sacrifice of living on the earth plane. In Heaven everything is perfection. Your soul reigns supreme, mind and body are still part of your essence; they are not forgotten, but the soul is the predominant force here.

When you are in the physical world of Earth, the soul is present; you are very aware of its presence but it is clouded by the body and mind. This is part of the human experience. Try to feel what your soul is; feel things from the top of your head to the bottom of your toes. Feel the vibration within you. Hear the hum, see the light. It's there, I assure you. Be mindful that it is an integral part of you. Without it you would not exist.

How do people connect with God?

Many paths lead to the connection with the creative force called "God." The path you choose is not at all significant to me. I hear and listen to every prayer. But it is within your own free will to make all things happen. I cannot "give" you anything. It's all from within. Many times I have heard your sweet voice talking to me. You never thought I could talk back! What joy I have in communicating with you. Ask your questions. I will try to provide the answers in words you can understand. Words are just tools for understanding. But watch your feelings, your gut, your intuition, for these can often provide you with tremendous information.

Trust that intuition, it's almost always right. I sense your wish to communicate with those who have passed on. Many have this desire. Do not let fear cloud the experience. Just as you're getting "it," fear will dispel the experience and your communication will cease. Have a consciously open mind and heart, and the communication will occur effortlessly. You can do this for others as well, for it is your desire to do so. Discovery is just around the bend. Be patient, dear one. Soon.

Should I be telling others of my experience?

Yes, my child. Tell all those who express an interest and wish to hear what you are experiencing through our communication. Do not try to convince anyone of its validity. Not all can grasp it. That's all right. All paths to God are correct and beautiful in their own right. All are truths for the individual believing in them. Love and kindness are paramount to every religion, the individual beliefs are inconsequential. God is one, man is one. Under the beautiful sun shine all people of every race, color, and religion. Their beauty is so diverse and individual.

Unity of all mankind will be possible when people realize that *all* religions are "right." They are the "truth" for each individual. Whatsoever you believe is whatsoever you choose to experience. *You* create that experience and it is *your* truth. If you believe you are going to hell, then you absolutely will create that hell for yourself. Quite silly, really. Why would anyone create a hell for themselves? It is derived from fear. Fear is what keeps you from reaching true inner peace, light, love—all things.

Live your life filled with love at all times, and surely you will create a Heaven on Earth as well as in the afterlife. If you can remember that love in the next life that you experience (difficult to do as it is deep in your subconscious) then your soul's progression will begin to accelerate. Fill your heart with love. Make that connection with the divine. Feel it. Live it. Be it.

Why is there so much human suffering?

The reason suffering exists is that without it, true bliss could not exist. Good-bad, yin-yang, alpha-omega, happy-sad, et cetera—all extreme opposites in nature are necessary. If you did not know and experience one, you could not have the other. Again I tell you that my greatest desire is to experience life on the beautiful Earth that I have created.

Through you, my dear children, I am able to experience it. This experience encompasses everything that is possible. Part of that possibility includes great suffering by many. Every soul has suffered to different degrees in different life-times. It is part of life as you know it. In fact, I reiterate that the life you choose to lead is of your own accord. You choose your birth parents and circumstances for each incarnation. I realize this concept is difficult for you to understand with regard to suffering. Why would anyone choose to be born into a life of great suffering? I cannot express in words sufficiently that your progression is relative to suffering. How else could you know to appreciate the simple wonders of life on Earth?

Some people walk around blindly, not rejoicing in all that they have. They want more, more, more. More material things, more intelligence, more beauty, more money, more possessions, more happiness. To know that you have all these things already is to have reached a point where suffering is unnecessary. You are very close to that point, my dear one.

I hear your prayer—I know how grateful you are for your existence, and the beauty of it. That despite its ups and downs and struggles, you have a wonderful life. You have suffered greatly in past lives, you have remembered in your subconscious those experiences.

In effect, the suffering all of mankind experience in their own lifetimes is the very hell many speak about. This hell could never be in the afterlife, it is on Earth. In the afterlife there is no suffering whatsoever. It is very difficult to explain the wonder of this place you name "Heaven." I will try to explain it when the question is asked. For now we are talking about suffering. Plain and simple, it is necessary for your progression. I cannot stop it or control it, but you can. Appreciate all that you have. Stop and smell the roses on a day-to-day basis.

Realize that those who cannot walk, who are blind, deaf, or have illness, are not necessarily unhappy human beings. They often appreciate all the wonderful things they do have and are able to experience. It is in this appreciation that they do not need suffering anymore. If you get lemons, make lemonade. Make the best of your given situation. It will get better (if that is your choice), if not in this lifetime then in the next.

Realize that people who are miserable in their hearts and in their lives choose to be that way. They create their own misery, and in some strange profound way that is what they need. Their problems seem to be so numerous, one after another—health, financial, emotional. They are very needy people. In their neediness, other people are attracted to them, good souls wishing to help. They can be helped, but only if they truly want to be. They can change their lives in an instant, but only if that is their choice. Tap into that love source. That is the greatest message I can give to you. For if you are able to truly do that, live it, be it—every day—then the suffering does not have to exist.

This sounds so simple, but it is the most difficult lesson for all people to learn. You are able to do this some of the time, but not all of the time. You know when it is happening, because no matter what comes your way you deal with it with a loving heart. When you act this way your body feels somewhat lighter, colors are prettier and more intense. You feel calm and centered.

Concentrate on how good you feel despite the actions around you or your own circumstance. When Christ was dying on the cross, he did not cry out in pain, because he did not feel it. His heart was so filled with love. This is true of all great spiritual masters. In all accounts by others, they suffered greatly but they endured effortlessly. They did not experience pain in the way we would think, because they were living lives of love. All the time.

They were so connected with loving energy that nothing could harm them. No suffering could be endured by them. Suffering could not exist. Many saw this as miracles of God. They were miracles of the soul. Their purpose was to show others love and its greatest beauty. Unfortunately, this message got somewhat distorted. Again—live a life of pure love. Try!

What is the role of animals on Earth?
Do animals have souls?
Can a human reincarnate into an animal?

When I spoke of the great mirror that I smashed, sending forth pieces of myself (billions of souls), there were also dust fragments left behind. These are the mini-souls of the animals. They are not as complex as the souls of humans (human souls also vary in their complexity). Their ability to evolve is limited because they are merely "dust" souls. But they are very important to the world and the complexities within it.

Their role is to serve mankind—for sustenance, for friendship, for assistance in making a living. Just because they are here to serve man does not mean they are to be used freely. They should not be wasted for reasons of gluttony or vanity. They should be treasured, admired, and appreciated. When man kills an animal, it should serve a purpose that is altruistic in nature. These precious creatures should not be wasted unnecessarily.

With regard to a human soul reincarnating into the body of an animal—this is possible, but there are few animals walking the Earth with human souls. Mainly this is because not much is gained for the soul from an evolutionary standpoint. But it is possible, if a soul desires it. It is definitely possible. When a soul chooses to have a lifetime as an animal, it is merely to experience it from that viewpoint.

Sometimes souls will enter the life so that they can be with someone they were very close to in life on Earth. They are able to be a companion for the remainder of that person's life on Earth. That is why, for instance, when a widow shares her home with a cat or dog, often soon after her death, her beloved pet dies. Their mini-mission on Earth has been completed. Enjoy all God's creatures, great and small. Treat them with love and kindness, and if you use them for the sustenance of your physical body, do not do so wastefully. Savor the sacrifice they have made for you.

Is there a "wrath of God"?

No. There is no wrath of God. This is the biggest misconception about God. What purpose would it serve? I have only love for all my people. I do not punish for "sins" committed by man, because to me there are no sins of man. The reason I created man was to experience my self on Earth through them. God is all things good, but for man to know what all things good are, he must experience what all things good are not as well. It is a hard aspect to understand, and I realize this. All souls are on a progressive path to all things good and loving. It is through each lifetime of experience that they learn and gain knowledge. The soul eventually realizes that good things like kindness, compassion, understanding, service, charity, et cetera, all service the soul in the best way possible for its progression. Some souls get this more quickly than others. Some ricochet back and forth, not making much progress. The key is in remembering (from your subconscious soul) that this is your true mission—all things good.

The terrible atrocities that affect humankind are, believe it or not, brought on by the great masses of people. They are also a necessary part of the natural law. The Earth can hold only just so many people or its complete destruction would surely occur. Cancer could be cured tomorrow as well as AIDS. All disease could be cured in an instant if that is what the great masses of people desired. But where would all these people live? Eventually a way will be discovered to relocate man to other worlds out in space. Then these diseases will all be curable. The ultimate goal is that of a physical world of pure love. When this happens, man's abilities will astound you. There will be no limits to what can be done. Life on Earth will be as life in Heaven. You are a very long way from this.

All of the "acts of God"—flood, tornado, earthquake, all natural disasters—are also brought about by the great masses. The negative energy that flows from humankind is transferred to the elements of nature. Misuse and abuse of our natural elements and resources has its cause and effect and operates under this law. Man cannot waste land, water, or air, without Mother Nature crying out and reacting in some way. Natural disasters are the reaction. They are not brought about by God. It is within the people's control. If the Earth is cherished, loved, and appreciated for all its beauty within and by all who inhabit it, then all natural disasters would cease. Again, it is within your control. Man is making some progress in this regard. There are new laws regarding conservation and pollution. They are steps in the right direction. With ever-expanding technology, ways and means will be found to reverse the damage done to the Earth mother. This requires time. How much time is in the people's hands.

With regard to the violent acts committed towards one another, unfortunately, this is part of the nature of man. Remember, for all things good to be experienced, the opposite must also be experienced. Throughout history, people have committed acts of such violence that gentle souls are appalled at what their fellow man is capable of. You, dear child, cannot even bear to read the paper any longer for all the violence in the world around you. You are a gentle soul, on the path to all things good. Many souls have not reached this phase of evolution. But you were once there as well. Remember that and be patient with the others. The violence is not greater in these days and times than at other moments in history. Actually, things are getting better. A shift is beginning to occur. A very slow shift, but one all the same.

Modern technology in the "information age" has enabled man to know what is going on in every far corner of the world. There is a much greater awareness of the violent acts committed by man. These acts are not becoming more frequent; there is just more awareness about them. This is a good thing. With awareness comes the desire for change. This is where the great shift towards nonviolence takes place. Someday, many thousands of years from now, violence will cease to exist. How long it takes depends completely on man's desire to *create* a world without it.

Is there alien life in other worlds?
Do aliens have their own God?
Do they have souls?
If so, are they the same as man's soul?

Yes, absolutely, there is life in other parts of the huge universe. You share the universe with many other forms. They have the same God as you. There is only one God, one creative force operating in the universe. The souls that inhabit the bodies of "aliens" from other worlds are the same souls that inhabit the body of humans. These souls have made a conscious decision to enter into these other worlds. There is a big universe out there. Picture a huge beautiful beach as a beach of knowledge and experience. Your experience is only one mere grain of sand from that beach. In your many, many lifetimes you will experience it all. Everything that you choose to experience is your decision, including the body or form you reincarnate into and the world that body inhabits. Time is also a factor here. This is going to be very hard for me to describe in words.

Here goes: Picture time as a great circle, with no beginning and no end. In the spirit world, time does not exist at all, but in the physical world, time does exist. When you reincarnate, it can be in any time you wish. It's just one big circle. Most souls choose to continue their progression of lives in an order that coincides with the linear unfolding of time as you know it. But the aliens you speak of are coming from a place that you call the future.

In many ways they are intellectually and physically more advanced than their human counterparts, but their souls are also at different levels of evolutionary process. Most come here exploring with good intentions to gain knowledge of this world. They do not realize that they have had past experiences on the earth plane. Their conscious minds have forgotten this, just as man's conscious mind forgets what lives it has experienced. These alien souls are also working towards the path to all things good. Do not fear them; most are closer to the path of good than the great mass of humankind.

Eventually there will be no discrimination towards people of different races, cultures, religions, or human species. By "human species" I mean that "aliens" and "humans" are of like souls. The progression of these souls is towards an understanding of all the various forms that a soul can experience within itself. Aliens will seek knowledge about the human form because they are fascinated by human existence. They realize that they are technologically far ahead of the humans on Earth.

They see the abuse of this planet Earth and are trying to understand and learn from it. Ultimately, they wish to help us in our need for healing this great planet of ours. They are intrigued by us. They do not realize that we are far more alike than different. They will take humans for observation and study, but they will not harm them in any permanent, significant way. They return these people gently back into this world with no conscious memory of what has occurred. The subconscious holds these memories, and they are accessible if one desires to remember. "Abduction" does not occur to very many people. There are many more claims of being abducted than actual occurrences.

Alien beings do not "take" humans from our earth homes frequently, because they have great respect for our privacy. This respect for our privacy, and knowing that many would fear them, are why there is no real "proof" of their existence. They know that the great masses of people on Earth are not ready to be aware of their existence. When the great masses are ready to acknowledge them, a new scenario will be created by human forms and alien forms. The meeting will be very exciting and transforming to our world. It may occur whenever the great masses of people decide it is time.

With this answered question, I began to realize that this is not my imagination, this is very, very real. Something wonderful is happening. The next few days were extraordinary. I arose each evening with new questions to ask. Every time I awoke, it was the same thing—a question would pop into my head and I would hurry downstairs to write down the answer.

Some nights several questions came to me. I did not stop writing until I felt satisfied that God was done for the evening. Every night that I awoke, I felt more alive than I ever had in my entire life. I felt completely at peace and filled with love. The dreary little room in my basement where I worked seemed brighter, cheerier than normal. I would usually fall into bed to sleep for an hour or two before getting my children up for school. When I went back to sleep, the sleep was deep and extremely restful. I awoke feeling incredibly refreshed and full of energy. I'd not yet told anyone of these experiences. It was my big secret. I had no idea how people would react.

Certainly, they would think I was completely nuts. I was truly afraid to tell my husband, Giacomo. He has a skeptical nature regarding spiritual experience. He would never believe me. He might even really think I was crazy! Yet I knew that I could not keep it from him much longer. I knew that I would get "caught."

I believe in angels.
What role do they play in our lives?

Angels are very important entities. They are everywhere, present in your life. They provide guidance and help in times of need. When you are in the heavenly realm of existence, you have many relationships with like souls that you have developed in many lifetimes. Before you incarnate into a body on Earth, you ask one of these soul-friends to accompany you in your next lifetime. Being your friend, the soul is greatly honored and is very happy to accompany you. I should mention that on the continuum of time, eternity is forever. Your soul lives for eternity. Eternity is a hard concept for people on Earth to comprehend, but in relationship to eternity one lifetime is the blink of an eye. So, in effect, your soul-friend has agreed to accompany you for a blink of an eye—no big task. This soul friend can be considered your guardian angel.

Before you inhabit a new body on Earth, you tell your guardian angel what your mission on Earth will be and what you are trying to accomplish. Once you are on the earth plane your guardian angel looks out for your welfare, helps keep you safe from harm, and tries to guide you towards your mission. In addition to your guardian angel, there are angels all about you and everyone else walking the Earth. They are present for your protection, guidance, love—all things good. They are happy to help you with the simplest of tasks, like finding your car keys. All you need to do is ask for their help. Angels are my messengers, they are souls who have chosen to remain in Heaven (for the time being, anyway). They help me with my work.

The angels that remain in Heaven provide a bridge for many people between my creative force and the souls on Earth. The angels can travel easily back and forth from Heaven to Earth. They do not have bodies to encumber them. When you feel their presence, or actually experience them physically by hearing or seeing them, they will come to you in a form that will not frighten you and that you can understand. They may appear to be quite ordinary in human form. They can appear to be children, or animals, or a homeless person—whatever fits the situation. If you are comfortable with seeing an angel with wings, or a glowing presence of light, then you may also experience them that way.

Angels can also make connections with you in extremely subtle ways. The whisper of the wind, the ripple of a wave of water, the beauty of a perfect rose growing in a garden of weeds. Listen to my messages through the subtleties of nature. They're there. You may not have recognized the intervention of your angels. For instance, say you usually take a certain route while driving your car to a place you've been many times before. This day you find yourself driving a different route, on a different path to get there. Perhaps you've just avoided an accident that might have happened had you taken the usual path. Follow your intuition, for it is your angels speaking softly to you, keeping you from harm's way.

Do not become so frustrated when things don't seem to go your way. When you are delayed or sidetracked, think of it as a redirection by your guardian angel leading you to a safe path in which your soul can progress towards the greater good. This is your mission. How specifically you are to get there is an answer that your guardian angel can help you with. That is, *help* you. The true answer lies within yourself. You hold the key. Appreciate your angels, thank them. They love to hear your words of praise. Then they know that they are doing their job, and serving me in a way that pleases me greatly. Angels are from Heaven, they are pure love in its highest form. See their beauty, their wealth of knowledge, connect with them. They will help you and guide you towards your mission. For that is their mission!

Dear God, I am so grateful and feel so privileged to be experiencing this communication with you. I feel very special and fortunate to be gaining so much knowledge in this lifetime and at such a rapid pace. *Just weeks ago I prayed for your guidance in my spiritual growth. I knew you were listening, but I never imagined that you would talk back to me! That you would answer my questions so directly and simply. Thank you, thank you, thank you for this great gift! Now, please tell me why. Why are you allowing me to have this amazing communication?*

What am I to do with this communication?

It pleases me a great deal that this communication brings you great joy. You are on the right path, my dear one. You are discovering your true mission in this life. You are indeed fortunate to be able to discover that mission. Many Earth souls go through life blindly, not quite knowing what they are supposed to do. Well, my dear, this is the message you should spread to others: Humans are evolving toward a greater good. There is life after death—many lives. I listen and hear every prayer, but the circumstances of each human's life are within his or her own control.

You create your destiny and the life you choose to lead. Your soul is constantly evolving and growing with each lifetime, with all hopes of moving toward all things good, of pure love. This evolution takes place faster for some and slower for others. Spread this word, tell people that the world is not in a state of hopeless despair. It can be fixed. It *will* be fixed. For it is within the power of each human being, through the use of free will, to create a world of harmony—a world free of suffering, free of discord, free of all evils. This world will someday exist; there is great hope for the future. There will be great changes among the people to produce this effect. Unfortunately, to fully understand all things good and loving, experiencing all things not good and loving is part of the progression. The souls of Earth forget their mission towards the greater good of pure love.

You are at the threshold of a new revolution—a spiritual awakening of humankind. This will not be a religious awakening, but, I stress, a *spiritual* one. All religions lead to God. It is not the individual message that is important. These messages are like mythology, they are symbols of what God represents. Because of the diversity of these symbols, wars are fought. These wars are pointless and do not bring forth any progress in the soul's work. People are slowly changing their ideas about religion and are understanding that all religions are one, united with one common God. There is a tremendous growth of interfaith and spiritual centers that bring people of varying religious backgrounds together to reach an understanding that all beliefs are beautiful, special, and the individual *truth* of the believer. All beliefs are valid and important to the individual, *but* they all contain the same message. Love one another. Every day live a life of pure love.

Consciously move towards that goal. It is within your reach. Create it. Make it real. God is patient. God is kind. God will wait forever for his blessed children to reach this goal. Meanwhile, send this message forth. Give it to all who will listen with an open heart. If you profit financially from this message, that is okay, for you must create a "living" for yourself. Why not make that living of service to God? It is all right to do that. I give you my permission. And please continue to ask your questions. For there are many left unanswered. I will continue to communicate with you for the rest of your life. Do not worry that the communication will cease.

After asking God this question I was tremendously relieved that I was told to spread the message to others. I simply could not contain my secret any longer. I was also unbelievably relieved and happy that God told me our communication would continue for the rest of my life. This was not a question I asked directly, but it was on my mind. God, of course, knew this without my asking.

That very morning I received the answer to the question, should I tell others of my experience? My husband woke up at about five A.M. to find me working at my computer. He asked, "What are you doing up?" I sat there with a ridiculous smile on my face. He asked, "What are you smiling about?" I still smiled. He asked again. I told him he would never believe me. I think he said something like, "Try me." I told him, "I'm having a communication of the most wonderful kind!"

Boy! He had no idea what I was talking about. I blurted out the whole story to him, about what I had been doing for the last several nights. The whole time, he just stood there looking at me. I asked him, "Do you think that I am crazy for believing I am talking to God?" He said, "Honey, if anybody can talk to God, you could!" I can't even begin to tell you my relief! My secret was revealed! It was as if a great burden had been lifted from me. And my husband didn't even threaten to have me committed. Soon, I thought, I will tell my family.

That afternoon I walked the short distance to my parents' house. I had my writings in my hand. As I walked the eight or so houses between us, I admired the beauty all around me. I marveled at the fresh, new, green leaves hanging from the springtime trees. A gentle breeze was blowing. I felt truly invigorated. Then I began to think about my intentions, why I planned to visit my parents' home that sunny afternoon. I started to think, "Maybe I am crazy . . . God, am I crazy?" I got a loud "No!" in my head. Oh boy, now God was talking to me in broad daylight as I walked down my street. I was very nervous and excited about showing someone in my family my answered questions. I figured, whoever I run into first will be the first one to read it. When I got there, no one was home! I could not believe it. Maybe I wasn't meant to show anyone quite yet. I went inside, thinking I would maybe wait just a *few minutes to see if anyone came home. In the next minute or two my mom walked in. She was exhausted. She had just done her weekly food shopping, a chore she hates more than cleaning the toilet! I said, "Mom, please, I want you to read something I have here." She said she was too busy. She had all the groceries to put away. I told her that if she would go into the living room and quietly read what I had, I would take care of it. It was an offer she could not refuse.*

As I put everything in its proper place, I kept having doubts. I kept thinking, "What is she going to think? Will these words speak to her in the way that they have spoken to me?" It seemed like an eternity before she came out of that living room. Surely, she must have read it more than once. When she emerged she was very quiet. She did not say too much. I really was not sure what she thought. She told me she wanted to show it to my father. I left the pages with her, not really knowing what she thought.

I later returned. My mom, dad, sister, and brother-in-law were all there. I asked my dad to read it. While I sat just a few feet away from him, I watched his expression. I tried to decipher what he was thinking. I tried to figure out what his response was. He did not say a single word until he was completely finished. When he finally spoke, he had tears in his eyes. He was utterly without words. He was very moved. I was so unbelievably happy! I knew then that I was not crazy. I knew these words are of utmost importance and relevance to our lives. I also knew that things would never be quite the same again.

God, I know we have addressed human suffering and that it is part of life on Earth, and often of our own creation. But please, dear God, explain to me why a young child suffers a horrible death of cancer, why a teenager is brutally raped and murdered, why a father is shot to death by a madman on a train?

Why do atrocities occur?

We established that human suffering is essential to the evolution of the individual soul. It is also part of a very complicated evolutionary process for souls that group together in a lifetime. Remember that even a small child dying, suffering horribly of some terrible disease, is not taken from the Earth by me. That dear soul made a decision before incarnating into that body, that its life on Earth would be short this time. I know it is very hard for a person on Earth to understand the desires and choices of a soul made on the other side of the veil—in Heaven. Life on Earth is a fleeting moment, so quick, so fast. A soul gains knowledge in each life that it chooses to lead. The progression of a soul is not always in the direction towards good. That is the ultimate goal. But it must experience all that is not good to get to all that is good. I know this is confusing, but it really is quite simple.

When I speak of souls that group together, it is a very deliberate grouping. They may have had great discussions of working together on this earth plane in Heaven before they were born into bodies here on Earth. Their arrival here is not by chance. Where they want to go and with whom has already been predetermined. Of course, these plans can change to a degree. Man has free will.

Often the suffering of one of the group's members (or more than one) will affect the group so profoundly that they will make great changes in their individual lives towards the greater good of man. For instance, the woman whose husband is shot on a train goes on to make great strides against gun control, to help end violence, as we know it. She is just one woman trying to make a difference. The brother whose dear sister was raped and murdered goes on to accomplish great things to help women protect themselves from the danger of violence. He gives women tools of empowerment to control their own safety—to create a world of safety for themselves. He is just one man and he has helped the lives of many, many women.

If the great masses of people chose to make a difference, it would happen so easily. In fact, all violence would cease to exist, if that is what the great masses chose to create. The small child sick and dying, suffering in his physical body, provides his family with comfort and love despite his great suffering. They are amazed at how this child endures. It literally breaks their hearts with grief. Yet their little one, so brave and strong despite all his suffering, inspires them. This precious soul (all souls are precious!) chooses to live a brief life ending in great suffering; he chooses to experience this kind of life. With this choice made and through this experience, the soul moves towards perfect love and all that is good in a very rapid fashion. This soul chooses to make a sacrifice in this short lifetime to move more rapidly toward the greater good.

Suffering also greatly affects the souls in the group who have gone through this lifetime with the soul that chose to depart. They now cherish life more than they ever could have before. They understand its sacredness and the true gift that it is. They miss their dear child with all their hearts in this physical life on Earth. But from a soul's viewpoint it is such a short moment before they are back together again in the beautiful kingdom of Heaven, rejoicing in the fact that there is no pain, no suffering, only pure love—so powerful, so joyous, so wonderful that we cannot imagine. It is one great party when these souls reunite in Heaven, and they have all grown from their experience on Earth.

The answers received through me had a profound effect on some of the people who read them. My father, whom I love very dearly, is happily one of the people who has gathered great insight through my experience. My dad never impressed me as even having a spiritual nature. I was quite surprised that the words spoken to me stirred something in him—something that needed to be awakened.

The day before his birthday I got a personal message,

23

*just for my father, from God. This was something new
to my communication. God was giving me a message
specifically for someone other than myself. I sensed
this was an important development. I felt that I would
be the channel for many others to receive messages.
Time will tell if I am right about this. The following is
the message I received for my father.*

My dear child, at this hour I do not want to provide you
with answers; I want to give you a more personal message—
one for your dear father, who gave you life. Because you chose
him as your father, he has been able to give you so much to
love and appreciate—the joy of nature and all its glorious
inhabitants, the sense of adventure and hard work, the idea
that money provides you with the ability to enjoy life but that
it is to be spent freely (more will keep coming). You didn't
even realize that he has given you some of these things.

You chose each other, as well as all other members of
your family here on Earth, with the hope of working towards
the greater good of man, of getting closer to pure love, which
will set your body-mind-soul free! This father of yours is having a birthday. It will be of great significance to him this year.
He will remember it forever more. This is because I have a
message for him: Enjoy life. Work is not all there is. When
you die you will have a life review. You will not look back with
great joy at all the business opportunities and experiences
that went with them. They are there and part of your life, but
they will be completely forgotten when you review your life.
What you will see is the joy you had with family and friends.
The times you took to be with one another, to love one another. The times you took together to quietly listen to the beauty of nature all around you. The times you celebrated and
rejoiced about all the abundance and riches you have.

Often this was at the dinner table. This father of yours
does enjoy his food! Tell him to think of the times he spent
preparing meals of love with his family members. Tell him to

concentrate and remember how he felt at those moments. He alone will know what I mean by this. This is one of the times he is happiest—when he feels almost comfortable enough within his own body to express his love to those around him. Another time is when he is doing the things he loves—like his great joy and love of the sea. This joy has been his since he was a small boy. This is the legacy that he will pass down to grandchild and yes, great-grandchild! He will live to be an old man. He needs time to realize what is important here on Earth in order for his soul to progress in his next lifetime.

When he arrives in Heaven he will be greeted by all those he loved in this lifetime and all the lifetimes before. This time the very first to greet him will be his beloved grandmother Marie. She loved him most of all. She sees all his beauty and all his glory and understands the pain in his heart. Tell him the pain can disappear at any moment he so desires. He is getting very near to letting that pain disappear. For it is not too late. Stop. Love your family. When you need to be with them, take the time to do so. Tell them that you want to have some time with them. Perhaps just an hour would make a great difference. Work is good for you and work is also your calling. But maintain a healthy balance between your life's work and your soul's work. It is the work of the soul that will also bring you great joy. You have been ignoring this work for too long. Stop. Take pleasure in the things that bring you happiness while you are alone. Enjoy the words the ocean and bay bring forth to you.

Listen to the silence, for in it are words sent to you from me, God. These "words" speak to you in ways that cannot be expressed to you here on this page. Have love in your heart, experience that love, do not be afraid of that love. As to love, your problem is fear. Fear of rejection. Fear of expressing that love to others. Get rid of this old fear, let it go. You will be so glad you did. And, my dear child, remember most of all that I, your God, love you most of all. It is to me you shall return. In this life in Heaven, you will know

25

what pure love is. It is within your ability to create a "Heaven on Earth." Happy birthday to you! I hope this message brings you great joy.

The evolution of man:
How did the human race get where it is today?

When the world was created, there was only land and water. Slowly, slowly life came forth. Tiny organisms began to grow and flourish in the great seas and on the warm earth. These tiny organisms were created by pure love, the love of God. These organisms grew and changed form into that of the great plants, trees, and all forms of vegetation. Slowly, slowly they grew and changed and emerged into the form of animals, animals that inhabited every far comer of the world, the seas, the land, the air. The animals had limited intelligence and intellect, but they were the purest forms of love, the love of God. Slowly, slowly these animals changed form and evolved into early human beings.

These humans were much more advanced intellectually than the animals. They were able to use their intelligence. Their world was based on survival of the fittest. Survival was not easy and man was savage. I, your God, wished to calm this savageness. I desired that this human take on a form capable of being aware of the pure love within him. This man had no awareness of this love. For he was just a physical body and mind. I wished to experience myself through this man I created, and in wanting to experience myself, I sent forth souls. At the moment of conception, when egg and sperm met, a beautiful, glorious soul entered the human being in a new life.

This new human man was quite different from his counterpart. This new man experienced life with an awareness of all things good and bad on this earth. These souls were of great innocence, for it was their first time ever on the earth plane. They had much to learn. The savage nature of man remained, for it was still an integral part of his existence. But slowly, slowly more and more souls entered the bodies of the new human race. And slowly, slowly man evolved. The evolution of the species is an ongoing phenomenon. Man is continually growing and changing, getting closer and closer to the greater good and living a life of pure love. This state of pure love I speak of is man in a state of existence that is utter perfection. Man has a great distance to cover before he will reach a state of perfection.

There are few individuals walking this Earth in this state of pure love, of perfection. Mother Teresa is a good example of someone who lived in your lifetime—one of your contemporaries who is the essence of this perfection. She surely will be named a saint in due time. Her life affected many and helped many on the path of perfection. You are all on this path. Some will get there more quickly than others. But this is not a race. It does not really matter how many lifetimes it takes to get there. Time is not a factor in the kingdom of Heaven. Time does not exist. It is an earthly condition. Perfection is within your grasp and will be attained by every soul I have created.

The human form is the sum of all things created before him by the pure love of God. In man's evolution he has been all things, tiny organism, plant, animal, and finally man himself. He was first a primitive man without a soul and finally, a human with a glorious soul sharing his body and mind. Three properties make up the new man: body, mind, and spirit. They are integral to human existence on this Earth. They are also integral to the soul's existence in Heaven.

When a person dies and his spirit ascends to Heaven, his body is left behind. It is a mere shell, an empty vessel, so to speak. In Heaven this soul is recognized by all those he encountered in his many lifetimes. The soul appears in the bodily form that the other souls recognize and loved most of all. So when you arrive in the kingdom of Heaven, you will recognize all the souls you encountered on the earth plane. You will see them in the form in which you knew them. And if you encountered them in many lifetimes, you will see the essence of every form they took. This is a hard thing for you to imagine and comprehend. Life in Heaven is a very complex existence indeed! We will talk of this more.

I feel so blessed to have two healthy children, boy and girl. This is what I always desired. You speak of having the ability to create "whatsoever you desire." I believe this to be true.

Why is it that two people who desperately want to have a baby cannot have one?

When a man and woman join in the sacred ritual of marriage, their greatest achievement together is often the creation of a new child made of their own flesh. This is their greatest desire, to reproduce a child of love. The desire is so great that they (more often the wife) obsess over the very thought of having this wonderful child. They plan and save their money, waiting for the perfect time to conceive this child. When they feel the time is finally right, they begin trying to conceive this child of love. Their fear that they will not be successful is great. What if they cannot have this child they so greatly desire? This becomes their only thought. Unfortunately, that which they don't want very much becomes exactly what they have. This is because they cannot think of anything else. They have put so much energy into this very thought that they have created it, they have made it real for themselves. I must mention that often a couple truly cannot have a child no matter what. They do not have the physical capability. Doctors may test and find something faulty in either husband or wife.

If this is the case, then it was a decision made by the soul in Heaven before it incarnated. This was a decision that in all likelihood was made together with their partner. If they have chosen their "right" partner in life on Earth, then that partner was chosen in Heaven beforehand. Remember, my children have free will and often they do not make right choices. Thus, so many "bad" marriages that don't work out. If you marry the person you chose before incarnation into this life, you will know it. Because despite the ups and downs and stresses of everyday life, you will find yourself blissfully happy and settled with the person you have chosen.

Sometimes the mind and body override the decision a soul made in Heaven. Their desire to have a child is so great, but perhaps they are not with their "soul mate" and believe that having a child together will bring them great happiness. Maybe it will. Even if you are not with your true soul mate, this does not mean you cannot have a happy life with the person you have chosen to be with in this world. There are many compatible souls who did not choose each other in the heavenly realm before life. Sometimes great progression of soul is made when two unlike souls are joined together in this world without their previous intention. These couples can give a good life to a poor child who has been rejected by his birth parents. If their great desire is to have a child, then they will find a way to make that a reality.

They will adopt. They will find a surrogate mother. They will buy a baby off the black market. They will somehow create the child whom they cannot physically create. Remember, all things are possible if it is truly your desire. In the case of couples who have no physical reason for their infertility, their inability to conceive this child of love is because of *fear*. They fear not being able to do so. They have given much, too much, of their energy to that which they fear.

They have created it. This can be changed if it is truly what the couple desires. First, they must stop fear right in its tracks. They must trust that God has given them the ability to have a child and that the rest is up to them. The ability is there. They must release the fear and make a connection with God. Concentrate on the connection, feel the love of the connection. Stop and appreciate all that is beautiful in the world. Relax and try to forget about the fear. This is a very hard thing to do. But until the fear is released, the child will not come forth. As soon as the fear is gone—often when a child is found through adoption—that is the very moment the couple conceives their own child, because they no longer have fear. The fear is released because they are finally getting the child they wanted so very badly and then—surprise!—they are able to produce one of their own flesh! What a glorious surprise. Now they have two children, both to be cherished and loved; both brought to them, "created" by the loving couple, in two different ways. Remember, create the desires of your heart. Release the fear. Make the connection with the divine love of God. Be aware of this enormous love. Feel it. Live it. Be it. Your child will come to you, somehow, some way, if that is truly your desire.

Why are some on a spiritual path toward enlightenment, while others choose to be in the dark?

All are on the same path. It is just that some have not remembered in their life on Earth that connecting with the light of God's infinite love for them is part of their true mission. Those on the path encounter many floundering souls on the way. They need your help in remembering their truest mission. Help them, dear child. Be kind to them. Be patient with them. Your infinite wisdom is a great gift to you. You were where they are yesterday and they will be where you are tomorrow. All are on the same path at different legs of the journey. But all are on the same great journey. Your ability to create as God creates enables your progression (and regression as well) on this path. You have no advantage over them; they can advance at any time on this journey and fly right past you! Remember this. For what you are helping them with today, they may be teaching you in the next day.

Treat one another in the way you want to be treated. Do no harm to another. When you have your life's review, you will experience from the point of view of another how you affected every life that touched yours. Whether good or bad, you will see it through their eyes. This is when you will have an opportunity to realize how you hurt others encountered while on the path. You will also experience the great joy you brought to others. In an instant you will feel every emotion of the lives of the many people whose lives you touched. This is quite an amazing experience! It is part of the beautiful transformation that takes place when the soul leaves the body and begins its ascension to Heaven. It is what people speak of when they say, "My life flashed before my eyes." In a true death of body it is much more pronounced and awe-inspiring than in a trial death in which spirit is abruptly sucked back into its body. This is the near-death experience many speak of. All who experience it are profoundly affected by it for the rest of their lives.

But this "near death" cannot even compare with the great wonder of "true death." For in true death, when the soul leaves the encumbered body, the most beautiful metamorphosis takes place, just like a butterfly emerging from the cocoon. The old shell of the body is left behind and the soul flies skyward. The experience is one that should not be feared. The love that you will feel will bathe you in the warmest light; it will envelope you with the grandest feeling. It will fill your every thread of being and you will vibrate with a resonance of the most beautiful sound. You will travel at the speed of light. You will become this light. This light cannot be described. It is love in its purest form. Do not fear this light. You will be pulled into it and then you will become one with it. As you become one with the light you will cross over to the kingdom of Heaven. You will be welcomed by all the souls you encountered and loved in all your lifetimes. Your joy in seeing them cannot be described. It is the most wonderful reunion imaginable. Do not fear this thing you call "death." It is truly rebirth.

You shall always return to God, your father/mother, the great creative force. This is your true home, and it is to this home that you shall always return. It is home where you are most comfortable and loved. Nothing but love exists in this place called "Heaven." No suffering, no regret, no turmoil. But in due time most of you choose to experience life once again. Your birth into this new life is equally as awe-inspiring and beautiful as the death from the previous. At the moment of your creation, when a soul enters a little tiny cluster of human cells, a light enters them. This light is your spirit. It is always and forever part of your existence on Earth and in the afterlife. It is the most integral part of your essence of being, no matter what form that being is in. Find your soul, be aware of its existence. Find what brings it happiness. In this happiness, this joy, you will find the greater good of man. This is what all souls desire and strive for: the greater good, a state of being in which only love exists. It is your soul's greatest desire to experience this state of Heaven (pure love) on Earth.

What is the intended role of parent to child?

When man and woman create a child, through the greatest physical act of love, that of procreation, they plant the seed of potential pure love in the ground of circumstance. Use the symbol of a sunflower. This little seed changes form and begins to sprout. It grows physically very rapidly. It always turns its face to that of the sun and its immense love for the tiny flower. The sun is a representation of the parent and the pure love for the flower. The flower grows and grows, and no matter where the sun appears in the sky the little flower seeks it out and turns its face towards that beautiful light. Be ye like the love of the sun, pure, enormous, unending. Your little flower will surely grow tall and strong!

The parent's role is one of so many, many things: first in giving life to that child, then in nourishing that life. The parent is the first teacher to the child. Everything that child becomes is a reflection of the parent's greatest intention. This is a huge responsibility, and not everyone is destined to play the role of parent. Those who are wise know this. If this little flower is tended to, it can grow to be six feet tall! It can surpass its parents' own growth. This little flower/child has tremendous potential for growth.

When I speak of this growth, I am referring to that of a spiritual nature. When parents aspire toward pure love and the greater good, their strongest desire is to bring forth children who are more spiritually evolved than they are themselves. All mankind has the inherent desire to follow the light of spiritual understanding and to allow the fullness of the seeds that grow from within to flourish. Child and parent have many struggles together. The child wishes independence, but is not independent. The child wants unconditional love, but learns that love on Earth has many conditions. The child wishes to develop his own set of rules, because he cannot live under the same roof with the rules of another. At this time, a parent must know when to set the child free—free to make his own mistakes, to create that which is not good, so that he may recognize good when he experiences it. If a mother (or father) has taken her job seriously and with reverence, she knows in her heart that the child will be okay. She knows that the child must be permitted to discover his own path in life toward fulfillment. The child will come back to her in due time. When that child returns he will have a new perspective and a new respect for the parent's true intentions. This is realized fully when the child decides to create a family of his own—or *not* to create a family of his own. He knows that parenting is the hardest job in life. Upon this discovery, child and parent experience a new closeness and understanding not experienced in the past. This is a great catharsis for all. A new love is born free from conditions.

Unfortunately, some parent/child relationships never evolve to this point. It requires wisdom and maturity in all parties involved. If you are successful in bringing your relationship with your child to this point, it will bring a great sense of accomplishment in this life with regard to your highest intention, your original plan of what a parent should be. The bonds between family members extend into the afterlife. You will be forever touched and affected by your experiences with your earth families. In Heaven all mistakes will be forgiven by all. What a joy it would be if these mistakes could be forgiven on Earth as well.

Each question answered has provided me with great insight into the mysteries of the universe and what God's role is in the great scheme of all things. These answers have also given me great insight on a very personal level. I found that many questions I asked were pertinent to what was happening to me in my life at any given moment. This makes great sense. Obviously, these are my truths, not necessarily everyone's truths. My hope is that the messages will bring insight to those seeking it, in the form in which I am expressing it. I hope it will also inspire those to seek out their own truths for themselves.

One question arose from a fight I had with my husband. It was really a silly, stupid argument. It actually was my fault. I didn't bring home dinner for my husband and son when I had said I would. They were totally furious with me. It was nine P.M. and they were famished. I felt really awful about it. My beloveds were so angry with me. I kept apologizing to my husband, but he was livid. Then I got mad at him because I thought he was overreacting. I went to bed very mad at him, something I don't like doing at all.

How can I learn to forgive others?

Forgiveness is grace. This grace will set you free from the pain and hurt you experience from another. Forgiveness is one of the greatest lessons you have to learn. When you acquire this ability to forgive, a great healing of your soul will occur. All wrongs will be righted. Understand that you have hurt others as well. Feel their pain, for you have caused suffering to others. This is not a bad thing. It is simply part of your human condition, of existence on the earth plane. You hurt each other. The simplest reason is that you seek power. In seeking to control others, you belittle, you act cruelly, you are sometimes even violent in your actions. Recognize that you have done all these things to those you love most.

Forgive yourself first. You are a mere mortal human being made of flesh. These are not your sins. This is your human condition, encumbered by body and mind. Your soul in its purest form forgives all. Connect with your soul. Connect with the pure radiance of light, of God's love. Feel the warmth, bathe in its greatest glory. Make the connection. Simply take a deep breath, relax, and choose to let your ill feelings go. As they fade away, rejoice in the fact that you can control your anger, simply change it. This sounds so easy, though I realize it is not. If you begin with just the desire to forgive, then forgiveness is just around the bend, because you create whatsoever you desire. Realize that forgiving others is a very "self-ish" thing to do. You will set yourself free! You will never feel better than when you choose to forgive. In your grace of forgiveness, others will realize the light in your eyes, the joy in your heart. They will say, "Why is she so happy?" You simply made the choice to forgive.

Your life is short, a mere blink of the eye. Do not waste time in constant conflict and turmoil. Especially let the little things go. If you make this a daily habit, it will be easier to let the big things go as well. I am not saying that you should allow yourself to be abused in any way. Empower yourself to create love in the hearts of those you wish to forgive, or those from whom you seek forgiveness. Fill your heart with love. Your everyday life will be affected greatly if you simply *try* to do this. You will have days when you are actually *able* to do this. Those days are the best! You float through them effortlessly. All conflicts are dealt with by a loving heart, a loving word, a loving action. People will notice the change in you. They may even think you're weird. But if you continue to fill your heart with love and act in a loving fashion, these very same people who called you odd will want to know what you have that they don't. Why is she so successful at running her life? Because her heart is filled with love *all* the time. You can do this!

Make an effort, it is hard work. I know this. Make an effort to try, and if you fail one day, start again. Each day is a fresh start. Begin with forgiveness of yourself, then your family members. One by one, forgive them. If you connect with the loving God and hold this connection, you *can* forgive. Your life will be so much better for it. If this can become a habit in your day-to-day life, a great transformation will occur.

Compassion will pour into your very being. It will overflow from you. When another person chooses to hurt you, instead of feeling angry with them, you will feel deeply sorry

for them. With this newfound compassion, you will understand. With this understanding, you will gain wisdom. With
this wisdom, you will have learned the great lesson of forgiveness. You will be set free!

*With this beautiful answer, I was able to com-
pletely forget my anger towards my husband. It simply melted away with these words of great wisdom.
God is truly so amazing! If everyone could just be still
and listen for this divine guidance, what a wonderful
world we would live in. I have since read this message
several times. Whenever I am angry with someone I
am able to peacefully let the anger go by reading it. I
truly hope that it helps you in this way as well. This
answered question left me feeling very inspired. I
responded to God, "Once again, dear God, I am so
very grateful for your answers."*

Why am I so blessed?

My darling child, *you* asked for this! *You* prayed for this.
I merely heard your prayer and answered it! I will talk with
anyone who so desires it. Whether or not they are willing to
hear my answers depends on them. In order to hear me they
have to first let go of any fear they have about communication. It simply won't work if there is fear.

Second, they have to have an unbelievable desire to experience and create this communication for themselves.
Remember, whatsoever you desire . . . you know the rest!
Third, they have to center themselves in a state of relaxation
and connect with the great energy and light of my enormous
love. It is this simple *and* this complicated! I will be speaking
with many, many others. I will have many, many mini-prophets
speaking God's word. The words will vary slightly so that the
message can get through and "speak" to each individual.

Your words will move many who read them. But it will
not be the message that leads to everyone's connection to the

great creative force of God. This is why I am speaking to many who desire this communication. Each message will have the same underlying truths, but there will be individual nuances in each communication that speak differently to different people. Do not be discouraged if your message does not "speak" to all those who read it. It won't. There is a message for them coming from another source. If they desire to hear this message, then it will come to them.

In the meantime, regarding *your* message, enjoy this communication and continue with it. It is important and certainly worthy of the attention you are giving it. Continue to write each day. I will continue to answer your questions. I will even help you in asking your questions. I love you with all my being, as I love *all* my children, every one.

I rarely read the newspaper or watch the evening news because is saddens me so deeply. Worldwide events are so distressing that I choose to bury my head in the sand. In the last year I have not been able to escape the news of the deaths of innocent victims. Children killing other children in calculated, brutal, cold blood. This absolutely scares me to death. If our children are not safe at school, where on Earth are they safe? The reason I am aware of these events is that despite the fact that I rarely watch the news or read the paper, these events are talked about by everyone I encounter.

Such tragic deaths affect young and old. They arouse strong feelings of compassion and empathy toward the families and the communities that have had to endure such tragedy. My son, who is an innocent child of eight, came home from school recently and told me that they had a minute of silence in school in memory of the poor children who suffered such violent deaths. It is my eight-year-old, Jake, who inspired this question.

Why are children killing children?

This is a condition that brings me great sadness. It appears to *not* be a movement towards the greater good of mankind. Yet it truly is. Remember, I spoke of all things good and all things not good. This is just what I am speaking of. To truly exist in a world of pure good, that which is not good must also be experienced, so that everything not good may be recognized. Then change may be created through the power of many, many people. Children are growing up in a different manner than a hundred years ago. They lack the supervision of a full-time mother, and often they don't have the presence of a father in their lives. The children who have committed such heinous crimes are in such great pain and turmoil that they have chosen this outlet to stop their pain, to cause the pain and suffering of others. Every one of them has been abused in their lives, either physically, emotionally, or sexually. When a child comes into the life of a parent, he needs the shelter of a parent's love. Many of these children are simply seeking shelter. As a result of committing these crimes, they are put away in a place where their basic needs of food, shelter, and water are met. Unfortunately, they never receive the love they are searching for. I call out to them, but they do not hear my call. If only they could hear me, they could make the connection with my divine love. Some will find me and their lives will change forevermore. They are mere children, children whose innocence appears to have gone, but it is still in their hearts. They acted so violently out of fear, fear of not being loved. This is a growing trend; it is not your imagination. What will happen is that just when humankind reaches its greatest moment of despair, great masses of people will seek to make a change.

Children are to be treasured, not thrown away like trash. Not everyone should be a parent. This is why man created abortion and birth control. The children who commit these violent acts are going to realize (if they haven't already), in their life review, the pain and suffering they caused others. In their next life they will move towards the greater good of man. This lifetime will have been extremely painful and they will have learned a radical lesson. In the afterlife they will be forgiven by even those they killed. It is human nature to make mistakes, enormous mistakes. Learn from them, big and small. If you can learn from them in your current existence, all the better. A small number of these children actually came from loving parents and families, but even these children have had some great pain and suffering inflicted upon them. Sometimes it has been self-inflicted. You are capable of torturing yourself like no one else can. These tortured children have sought to release their pain, but unfortunately it has been magnified many times. Why, you ask? Because they do not recognize God's love.

What will the new millennium bring to mankind?

Mankind will soon be living in a new age of spiritual awakening. There are many events signaling this change going on around you right now. Open a book, turn on the evening news—people everywhere are aware of it. A buzz is in the air. People have always been searching for their religious path. They are now seeking the path of spirituality. This is a new way of thinking. Interfaith organizations are widespread amongst the various religions. Priests, rabbis, ministers are all speaking to one another, talking of the universal truths among all religions. A realization will be made that these individual religions are beautiful and wonderful but are more mythology than absolute truth. This is big news to all! This news will be met with great controversy. The shift will take place over many, many years. But the shift in beliefs is now beginning. Mankind's progression is absolutely relative to the understanding that religion is important only because it brings many into contact with God in a way that is comfortable to them. The individual religions really are not important. What is of importance is that people make that connection. Arguing over which religion holds the truth is a waste of your energy. Man will soon realize this, and religion will be looked at as part of your family tradition and heritage.

A new idea will develop rapidly, based on the fact that God is one, man is one, and all religions are one. It will be realized by the great masses of people that all traditions lead to God and your religious background is simply part of where you came from. With this new spiritual awakening, man will become very much in tune with God. Connecting with God's love will be of utmost importance in everyday life. It will be realized that with this connection all things are possible. The more that people make this connection and radiate the love within to all those they encounter, the more they will be able to change the world. It is possible that violence will cease to exist, poverty will cease, suffering will cease, disease will cease. With love in the hearts of many, great things can be accomplished. With love in the hearts of *all*, *anything* can be accomplished.

Understand that this great shift in understanding will slowly take place. It will not be overnight. There will be great conflicts as a result of this shift. When many people reach a point where they will not tolerate the atrocities going on all around them, this is when change can be made. When two individuals get together, the energy level of both can rise to a much higher level. When great masses of people get together, the energy level is so high that they could literally move mountains if that is what they so desire.

The new millennium has been prophesied to be the end of the world. In a sense, this prophecy is true. There will be an end to the world as we know it. The new world will emerge over time. It will be a world in which all people work towards the greater good of man; where all people live with love in their hearts, all the time. It will be a world that you cannot now imagine or even comprehend. It is very difficult for me to express with words what this will be like. The new millennium is the beginning of this great shift. It will be looked upon as a great time in history, a golden age of awakening. Begin this shift with yourself. Radiate love to all you encounter. Live each day with a loving heart. With every decision you make, ask yourself, "Am I working towards the greater good? Do I have love in my heart?" If you can answer yes to this, change is imminent. With every life you touch, try to lift their level of "love-energy" up. Bring it up a notch or two. In turn the person you touch will automatically strive to do the same with everyone he encounters. Soon all will be lifting each other up to a new level. This will not be achieved in this lifetime. But it can begin in this lifetime. Remember, it is a progression. A progression that takes a very long time. The joy is in the journey, not the journey's end, as I have told you before. Enjoy the journey!

Why does homosexuality exist?

I have created many beautiful individuals. All serve as an important reminder that individuality is what makes the human being most precious and wondrous. Think of the colors of a rainbow—which color is more beautiful? There is no way that a single race, religion, sexual preference, or any other variation can be singled out as being more beautiful than another. I love all my people, all my beautiful children. If anyone tells you that a particular attribute of an individual person is inferior to that of another, they are wrong, wrong, wrong! These various attributes are what make the world so interesting. Imagine a world in which all people were of the same genetic, social, economic, and religious backgrounds. How uninteresting life would be. What would you talk about? I mean this in a humorous way. People find it very enjoyable to point out the differences they perceive about each other. With regard to homosexuality, this particular group of people is of utmost importance to the great scheme of things (as are all groups of people). First of all, they are not sinners, they are just in a minority. Minorities are unfortunately often looked at

43

as inferior by the majorities. This is simply the way the world operates.

Remember that in the eyes of God there are no sinners! I love all my children equally—scoundrel and saint. In fact, the scoundrels can sometimes be quite amusing to me. God has a wonderful sense of humor! Homosexuality is important to the evolution of man, as it is certainly a natural form of birth control. The love expressed between two people is expressed in many different ways. The manner in which it is expressed does not really matter. There is no right or wrong way of expression.

Human sexuality is a great gift I have given to you for your enjoyment and pleasure. I would not have given my children apparatus for play if I did not want them to play with it. The original plan was that sex was for procreation. So I made sex wonderful and delicious in order that procreation would be an easy task. And boy, did you ever procreate! Homosexuality is a natural way to express love without sending forth offspring. There is a need for this type of love, just as there is a need for heterosexual love. It saddens me to see that minorities (all minorities) are looked down upon by many people. Great hatred has arisen out of the hearts of many.

I am going to tell you something that you did not ask about, but I will tell you because it relates to homosexuality. I told you of the great power of great masses of people. With the combined energy of many, anything can be accomplished—good or bad. Sadly, many people believe that homosexuality is bad or wrong. This belief is based in fear. Fear of something different from themselves.

Because of this great fear, the terrible disease of AIDS was created by the great masses of people. It takes many people to create something so powerful and devastating. It will take great masses of people to eliminate this disease and all others. Think about whom this dreadful disease affects: homosexuals, drug users, those who are promiscuous. These are groups of people that the great masses fear. They believe them to be dangerous or evil. Sadly, this disease was created to eliminate these groups of people.

Many have been eliminated, many more will die. Throughout history great plagues have scourged the Earth. All have been created out of the fear of man. I realize this is hard for many people to believe. Many have believed in the great "wrath of God." But there is no wrath from me. Only love. If the great masses of people lived with only love and acceptance in their hearts, these diseases would never have a need to be created in the first place. Great changes in man's thinking will occur over time. When the great masses of people wish for all disease to end, it will. When acceptance of all God's beautiful children is achieved, disease will not have a place any longer.

If all disease could be eliminated and people lived longer, where would we put everybody?

Do not worry, dear one. Mankind is a long way from eliminating all disease. By the time the human race reaches this destination, they also will have made tremendous strides in many, many other areas. Examine the technological advances in the last several hundred years. It is hard for you to imagine what life would be like without electricity, the motor car, computers, flight—all wondrous creations of man.

These great achievements and discoveries were made over a very short amount of time. Merely hundreds of years. Imagine, if you will, what man can create over thousands of years! Mankind will branch out into the universe. Early explorers traveled the very earth you live on. Explorers of the future will travel the universe. They will set up habitats for themselves in far corners of space. They will develop a way to travel effortlessly from star to star. This is hard for you to imagine. But if your great-great-grandfather were told of travel to the moon, that would have been very difficult indeed for him to imagine.

There is plenty of room in the universe for man's growth. A time would come when the Earth would not be able to hold all its inhabitants. This will not materialize, though. Man will work it all out long before this could ever actually happen. The technology of tomorrow will surely amaze the man of today! The TV show *Star Trek* is not really that far-fetched. Whatsoever you can imagine is whatsoever you have the ability to create. Look at the early TV shows with the little flip phones, the laser guns—these have already been created and are being used by man. Everything you can dream of is possible. It is just a matter of time before these dreams are realized.

Man's progression is ever-changing. This progression is essential to the human condition of life on Earth and the condition of the soul's life in Heaven. Your body, mind, and spirit are constantly evolving and changing towards the greater good of man.

What is love?

Aaahhh, love. Love is the grandest of all states of being. My prophets, philosophers, poets, theologians, great leaders, the smallest of children, and many, many others—all have tried to explain love. Through the simplest of song and rhyme and the greatest symphonic masterpieces, mankind has tried to explain love. The greatest writers in all of history have tried to explain love. The greatest artists of all time have tried to express love through painting, sculpture, all manner of expression through art.

Love is the subject of the most metaphors ever written. Love is patient, love is kind, love lasts forever, love knows no boundaries, love is never having to say you are sorry, love is all you need.

There is nothing that can even compare to the attention that love has received from mankind. The love for your husband, wife, father, mother, sister, brother, newborn baby, child, grandparent, friend, lover, pet, your home, your many possessions. Your love for me, your God—this grandest of all states of being is many, many things. This is why it is *the grandest*. Love is all things good. It has many variations to suit many different needs.

Love is compassion. Love is kindness. Love is patience. Love is trust. Love is family. Love is acceptance. Love is hope. Love is faith. Love is unity. Love is appreciation. Love is tenderness. Love is passion. Love is fraternity. Love is beauty. Love is eternal. Above all, in its absolute simplest form, *love is joy*! Fill your heart with all these things that love encompasses. Your life will be blessed. Your soul will be blessed eternally.

> *My mother's father, Grandpa Frazer, was a very special man. He passed on five years ago. I have two sisters, and a brother who was born when we three girls were much older. When we were growing up this beloved grandfather of ours doted on us and loved us in a way that you cannot even imagine. He cooked our favorite foods when we came to visit. He had all our favorite snacks in the house.*
>
> *We played "princess" and he fed us ice cream in the bathtub. He insisted we sleep in his bed, while he slept in an old beat-up chair. When he tucked us in at night he would tell us stories literally for hours. And he would rub our feet for us tirelessly, until we fell into a deep, peaceful sleep. He was a very special man indeed. I don't know if any human being could have possibly loved us more.*
>
> *When he died at the age of eighty-nine, we missed him terribly. He was old and sick ready to be with "his Lord, Jesus Christ." He hung on for days. I came to him that last evening and said to him through my tears, "Grandpa, it's okay, you can go. We love you." That was the last time I spoke with him. He died early that next morning. My two sisters and I will*

*never forget the tremendous love he had for "his girls."
My sister Nicole became engaged on the third of July
in 1996. The following night was the fourth. I spent
it rather quietly with my family, watching fireworks in
my parents' backyard. It was a gorgeous evening. The
fireworks were particularly beautiful that year.*

*I went home feeling very content. My husband
and daughter went to bed. My son Jake and I decided to stay up and watch television for a while. I put
on a videotape about angels that I had wanted to
watch for many months and had never gotten a
chance to. Jake quickly fell asleep with his head rest-
ing softly in my lap. I sat there and stroked his light
brown hair. I looked down at my precious baby, not
believing how big he was.*

*As I sat there, I began to feel extremely relaxed—
in a state of meditation, for lack of a better word. I felt
very heavy, yet light as a feather. My arms were lying
in a crossed position over my chest. I felt that my arms
were so heavy that I could not lift my hand off my
chest. I thought to myself, "This is ridiculous—of
course I can lift my hand up." With that, I lifted my
hand. I looked down at it. It was glowing—brilliant
beautiful colors outlined every finger. I looked at my
hand with utter amazement. My exact thought was,
"Wow! That's pretty cool!"*

*The entire room looked so beautiful. I could see a
glow on everything in it. All my senses seemed to be
sharper than normal. I was enjoying the moment so
much. I did not want it to end. I had never experienced anything like it before. With that, from the far
left corner of the room a presence entered. I could not
see its form, but I felt its unbelievable beauty and energy. I could not identify who it was. In my mind, I
asked, "Who is it?"*

*With the question asked, I felt the spirit sit down
on the couch, at the end by my feet. The spirit laid its
hands on my feet and began massaging them!*

Instantly the tears began flowing down my cheeks, for I knew just who it was! Grandpa Frazer. He had a message for me.

I could feel his loving energy fill the room. I could sense his smile, his happiness. He told me, "I am so happy for Nicole!" He then told me, "I am at utter peace, I am with my God." He then vanished as quickly as he had entered. It was over so quickly. I almost thought, "Was I dreaming?" But no, I was very much awake. My child was sleeping, the dog was sleeping—even our cat was sleeping, all in the very same room. But I was very much awake! The room still maintained its glow. I sat there for at least thirty minutes taking in what had just happened to me. I thanked God for letting me experience such a blessing.

Nearly two years have gone by since this wondrous experience happened to me. My sister Nicole is soon to be married. I have asked God to allow me to have a communication with my grandfather.

Dear Grandpa Frazer,

I love and miss you so very much. Nicole is getting married in one week. What do you think?

Oh darling, I am so happy! Please tell her Buck is a good man. I like him very much. It will not rain on that day. It is the day that my baby girl first smiled at me. My honey bun. Your mother, Bonnie. I will be with you, and you will know it. I will give you a sign so that you know it. Watch for it.

I love you more than I can tell. I love you all so much and I miss you. I am in the most wonderful, wonderful place here with our Lord, Jesus Christ. But I visit you often, I am part of your everyday life. I see you more now than when I was in that nursing home. You just don't see me! Pay attention! I'm right here. Nicole, my hand will be on your shoulder as you walk towards the lighthouse.

I will smile down on you all day. I am so proud of you

and the work that you are doing. I knew you could do it! You have my gentle and strong hands. My love to everyone— please tell Bonnie and Anne that I love them more than I can tell, and tell Andrea that she has too many birds! (Ha! Ha!)

Tell Andrea and Petey and the little ones that I love them all more than I can tell. And when the sandman comes to visit each night, it's me, tucking them in. Now go to sleep my sweetie pie. Sleep tight, don't let the bed bugs bite! Remind Nicole she has the key to my heart and I know it.

XXXOOO
Grandpa

The next day I gave this message from my grand-father to my sister Nicole. It brought her so much happiness! She told me that just the day before she had experienced something "strange." She felt someone touch her on the shoulder. She expected to turn around and be greeted by some familiar face. But when she turned, no one was there. She thought at the time that it was Grandpa Frazer, kind of reassuring her about the upcoming big event.

I had no knowledge of Nicole's experience. When I received the message from Grandpa Frazer it was truly a confirmation of his presence in our lives. Nicole got married on June sixth, the day after our mother's birthday. It was an unbelievably perfect day. The sun was shining brightly, the temperature was in the seventies, there was a gentle breeze—not a cloud in the sky! It rained the day after. In fact, after the wedding, it rained for ten days straight. Some days there was just a light drizzle, some days had violent thunderstorms, but it rained every day. What a blessing it was that Nicole had such a beautiful day.

The marriage ceremony was performed under the Fire Island lighthouse, right on the Great South Bay—such a beautiful location that has so much meaning to my entire family. The reception was held at our parents' waterfront home. We really needed to have a beautiful day. It would have been disastrous if it had rained. But it did not rain. Grandpa Frazer promised us that it would not rain, and he always kept his promises. After the wedding and all the festivities were over, we realized the blessing of this wonderful day. We realized that the people present in our lives on Earth, the people who loved us most, are forever present in our lives. Death does not separate us. If we are still and quiet, we can feel their presence. If we can take a moment to relax and fill our hearts with love, we can connect with our loved ones who have passed on to the afterlife. If this is your desire, you too can make it happen.

Simply ask.

Can you tell me about ghosts?
Do they exist?
How are ghosts different from angels?
Can they do harm?

The "ghosts" you speak of are entities/souls/spirits who have difficulty leaving the earth plane and ascending into Heaven. They are in a state of limbo. They are souls who have left their bodies but have gone no further. They have not been able to let go of their earthly existence for whatever reason.

Sometimes this is because they had a very traumatic death, or they do not want to leave their loved ones behind in this life. When their spirit departs from the body, a great white light encompasses them. They run from the light. Most souls bask in the warmth of God's love and are drawn into this beautiful light. These souls flee. They are just not ready to leave this place called Earth.

Most souls do stick around for a little while before ascending to Heaven, they just want to make sure their loved ones are okay. But a ghost is a transient being; it does not belong here, and it knows this but does not know how to get to the other side. They aimlessly walk the Earth not knowing what to do. They often make quite a nuisance of themselves. They need your love to make the journey to Heaven. Do not fear them. They cannot harm you. But they can frighten you, if you let them.

Fear is a very powerful thing. If you ever encounter a ghost, send it your love-energy and ask it to move on its merry way. Tell it that God is calling it, that its loved ones are awaiting their arrival. Sometimes they just need to be reminded of this. Ghosts will not be perceived by those who are not in tune with their subconscious, spiritual selves. So the people who fear ghosts the most will, in all likelihood, never have an encounter with one. If you have an open mind about this kind of encounter, it can be a beautiful experience. It is an opportunity to help a lost soul to the other side.

An angel is a different entity. Angels are souls who remain with the loving creative force of God. They are my little helpers; they are your little helpers. Remember, you are all little pieces of God. We are all one. Some angels have never experienced a lifetime on Earth. They have chosen to remain in Heaven to assist souls in their lives on Earth.

Ghosts, on the other hand, are not there to help you. They need help themselves, from you and from the loving angels. The angels can intervene and assist in bringing them home to God.

Communication can occur between you and an angel and also between you and a ghost. Angels can take on the form of anything they desire; they come to you in a form that is most comfortable to you. If you wish to see them with wings and a flowing robe, this is how you will see them. It is possible to have an angel come to you as animal, child, an intuitive thought or feeling. Ghosts will appear as residual energy of what they were in this life. If they are the ghost of someone you knew, it is possible that you will recognize them. Depending on how clairvoyant you are, you may be able to see, hear, smell, or feel these ghosts that walk the Earth. If you request to have an encounter with someone who has passed on, and that soul comes to you, it is just that—the "soul" of your loved one.

You may think of such souls as angels, but they are distinctly different from my other angels. There are so many fine details that cannot be explained regarding the hierarchy of souls in the kingdom of Heaven. Trust that these souls have a presence in your life. Have faith that you have many, many angels who guide and protect you. Do not fear ghosts; rather, assist them in reaching the glorious place all souls call "home."

How often do souls typically return to Earth?

Some souls have never experienced life on Earth. They are quite content to exist in a place of pure love and joy. They have no urge to experience that which they already know. But many souls do wish to experience everything there is. All extremes of existence. To truly understand pure joy, they need to experience it all—everything good, bad, and in-between.

There is no typical measure of how long the interval is between lives. But the average is about two hundred years. A lapse in this much time allows the soul to experience life in an ever-changing world. This is a sufficient amount of time for great changes to occur. It also allows souls to welcome the people closest to them in life on Earth to the afterlife with open arms. They will not incarnate into a body until all their offspring and often several generations after have come to the other side. In the grand scheme of things two hundred years is a very short time. On Earth it seems so very long, but in Heaven time does not exist as it does on Earth. So these two hundred-odd years are an instant. Some souls walking the Earth have been here hundreds and hundreds of times. Others are walking the Earth for the very first time.

When an infant is born into the world he is still consciously connected to the memory of his soul. This memory is very quickly forgotten. By the time the child is six months old there is no longer any conscious memory of his previous existence. Newborns arrive into the world with all the spiritual knowledge they wish to possess. The child almost immediately forgets what this knowledge is and then spends the rest of his life trying to remember that knowledge.

You are very aware of this great knowledge that newborns possess at birth. This is why you adore them so very much! They appear to have a luminosity so beautiful. Their beauty brings tears to your eyes. They have been so far untouched by the harshness of the physical world. Their innocence and their wisdom are incomprehensible. That glow you see is not imagined. That connection you perceive with the higher power of God is not imagined. A newborn child is truly a miracle right before your eyes, each and every one.

Does time exist in Heaven?

Time is a condition only on Earth. This is a difficult concept, but let me try to convey a message. The physical world needs time for many reasons. It is a gauge of your progress and growth. Without the passage of time, you would not be able to continue changing and evolving. Most are born in a state of perfection. Newborn babies remember pure love, because that is where they most recently came from. In a short amount of time they forget this. They grow physically, mentally, and emotionally. They learn and experience all that life has to offer. At some point they ask themselves, "Is there more to this life of mine? What is my purpose? Why am I here?"

Some ask these questions of themselves in early adolescence, others in middle age, others on their deathbed. These questions begin their quest for knowledge of a spiritual nature. They are now trying to remember what pure love is. It is God; so they are searching for God. Many find me through their religion. This is why religion plays an important role. As I have said before, choice of religion does not have any significance. However you find me does not matter. I speak through many channels. I am speaking through you right now!

I speak through nature: the beauty of a snowflake, the smell of a rose, the taste of honey, the wonder of a sunrise, the howling of the wind, the perfection of the changing seasons. I speak through my many prophets who try to convey the love of God. Great scripture has been written and produced by those trying to convey the love I have for my people. Some of the scare tactics used in the scripture of many religions are necessary because they enable people to work towards the greater good.

All mankind has the ability and inherent desire to work towards that greater good. Some require hearing a message that portrays God as vengeful and all-powerful, a God who places judgment on all. This gives them a moral conscience. Some people do not need religion to find their conscience. This does not make them sinners! They find God through other means. Some find God through their life's work. These are the caregivers of the world: the teachers, the doctors, the firefighters, and the marriage counselors. Some find God when they create a child of their own. They are so profoundly affected by the love of their child that they realize, "Oh yes, there is a God!"

Some never find God in their life. This is a sad fact. Some go through their whole life never recognizing the perfect love of God. These souls return to Earth again and again to experience all that there is, and to remember where they came from. When they return to me they immediately know and remember what that enormous, all-powerful love is. But the greatest joy is to find and experience that love through the physical existence of life on Earth. Not all souls desire or need to experience this existence physically. They are contented souls, with a desire to forever remain in my light.

It is true that in Heaven there is no passage of time. It is not necessary to gauge one's progress in this existence. There is no progress to be made in a state of loving perfection. Time stands still. Each moment is the now. Souls can enter your world and watch you live your life and in the very same instant they are existing in that pure light of God's love in Heaven.

Does a soul retain any of its human qualities?

If you mean, does it keep its personality? Yes! It keeps only its very best qualities, though. Whatever attributes were of a loving nature are kept. Anything that is not of love is discarded. But if a person was a practical joker in life, he will still be a practical joker on the other side. If a person is serious, he will have a serious soul. If he was always positive, this is retained and kept. If he brought joy to others and love to others, it is true for his existence in Heaven as well. The personality of an individual soul is retained from lifetime to lifetime. It can change to a degree, if the individual desires to make a change. You can make a conscious effort to change your personality in life. This is part of your free will to create whatsoever you desire. So if you see the glass as half-empty all the time but this is not what you want to be, you can alter your perception of things. In time you will have altered your personality.

You will meet souls on the other side. Suddenly it will become quite clear to you who they were in life, in whatever way you loved them most. This is how you will "see" them. So if your mother was most beautiful to you at age thirty-three, this is how you will see her. You will also be aware of their other lives on Earth. You will suddenly perceive that which they were in all their lifetimes. You may also realize that you've been together before. This realization will be very amusing to you. There is a realization of so many great mysteries when you arrive in the kingdom of Heaven. All questions will be answered. All great mysteries solved.

Part of why you feel the inclination to keep returning to life on Earth is that there is no awareness whatsoever. You go through life *not* knowing all the answers. It is the element of surprise that so delights you. You have forgotten everything of your existence in Heaven. You spend your entire life trying to remember. In trying to remember, you experience all the wonderful ups and downs that life provides. If you are on a spiritual path, you will receive mere glimpses of what it is you are trying to remember. If you are truly tuned in to your spiritual self, you will experience moments of Heaven on Earth. These moments are the most joyous to experience. They give you the most pleasure. They make life worth living. All the "bad" can disappear if you experience these moments of great joy and love. Even if they are fleeting moments, their memory stays with you for a very long time. The memory sustains your sense of hope that you will again experience these moments I speak of. *You* yourself know which moments I am talking of.

A personal example is when you are at the beach with your dear husband and children. It is a beautiful day. The sun is high in the sky, it warms you. You can actually feel the love of the sun. There is a gentle breeze softly caressing you. The air smells wonderful. You taste the saltiness in your mouth. You hear gulls calling to each other in flight overhead. The great ocean that you love so very much is calm this day. The waves gently roll in one after another. You dip your toes in the cold water. You feel the sand rush around your feet as you stand in the water; your feet are soon buried. You are the only people within one hundred yards of the beach. Your children are being loving to one another, helping each other build a sand castle. Your husband is fishing, he is at peace.

You are living in the moment and almost wish you could press the PAUSE button. You are having a joyous moment of pure love. Love for everything around you. You feel very connected with the divine source of God's love. You say a silent prayer of recognition, thanking God for giving you this moment. I hear your prayer. It brings me great joy when you acknowledge and appreciate these moments. Later, when your children are fighting and your husband is complaining because the dog threw up on the couch, you remember your moment and its memory stays with you. You take a deep breath and deal with your everyday existence until you can experience another moment once again. It is these very moments I speak of that bring you back here again and again.

Back to experience the wonders of your physical being. It is Heaven to which you will return. For you belong home with your God. But it is to this great Earth that you will return to vacation!

Is there power in prayer?

There is undeniably great power in prayer. When even a small group of people join together with the intention to help someone, through their prayers, the intention—the prayer—can very often be realized just because they will it to be. When a large group of people get together, the combined energy level is so great and powerful, their prayer gets results. Dear children, you must always be careful for what you pray, because you very well may get it! Recently there was an amazing occurrence. Seven babies were born to a young couple. These babies were truly miracles. They will all survive and flourish. The reason? The power of prayer. Many, many people prayed for these tiny infants. These people prayed with great intent and the belief in their prayer. This is why these babies lived!

The entire world you inhabit is made of pure light energy. This includes everything—the rocks, the soil, air, water, all the natural elements; all the animals, all the plants, great trees, and all manner of vegetation. The multitudes of people are all made of this pure energy. All this energy interacts. It is really one large mass of energy moving and changing form. But it is universal. Everything is connected. Your thoughts and feelings affect everything in this world you live in. Negative and positive energy flow continuously. There is a relationship between these energies—a give-and-take. For every action there is a reaction. You can alter the world by your thoughts as much as by your actions. If you send someone positive love-energy, they will feel more positive energy within themselves. If you have a connection with the divine energy of God, you can pass this energy on to another. You know what this feels like. You have uplifted others with your good intentions, with the connection of God. Your feelings of love are radiated to all you encounter. Your feelings of a negative nature are also passed on to others and the world around you.

You should be aware of the impact this can have. This is the great power of the great masses of people. The negative energies alter the very essence of the universe. All of the great human tragedies in the world are created out of this negative form of energy. It has to go somewhere. It has to manifest itself in some way—through flood, fire, earthquake, great storms of all kinds. This is where all negative energy goes. This energy is very, *very* powerful. This energy comes from the hearts of many unhappy souls walking the Earth. This is why it is so very important to have a positive outlook and see the beauty and love in all things. If you look closely enough, everything contains this love. It is sometimes difficult to find, but it is there. If you can recognize and appreciate love, your outlook cannot help but be positive.

So every day make a concentrated effort to be positive, to connect with the wonderful, unending source of God's love. Pass this love on to everything you encounter. Not just people. Love the mountains, the sun and moon in the sky above, the water, the air you breathe. You will see the world in a new light. You will understand that you were only seeing with your eyes in the past. You are now seeing with your very soul.

The power of your intentions and your prayer is tremendous. It affects all you encounter. Small groups of people combined in their efforts of intention can often perform small miracles. Large groups of people can perform even larger miracles. The great masses of people, when working towards the greater good of man, can alter the world forevermore. So powerful are the positive energies of many people combined. It begins with the individual.

An individual uplifts many around him or her. This small group of people pass their positive love-energy on to a larger group. The larger group spreads out to the far corners of the world. This loving energy is passed onto many, many other groups. In time, the majority of people will emulate this positive love-energy at all times. The great shift will then have begun. Remember, this great shift begins with the *individual*.

Are abortion and capital punishment wrong?

There is no right or wrong, there is no sin, or retribution for sins committed. *But* there are all things that are good and all things that are not good. Certainly, killing is not good. God does not give precious life to humans with the intention of another human snuffing that life out.

Birth control is a practical creation of man. If individuals do not want to give birth to a life, then they should either practice a reliable method of birth control or they should abstain from having sexual intercourse altogether. Celibacy is the most reliable. You ask, what if a woman is brutally raped and a child is produced—what then? The woman should have faith that this child was meant to be a part of her life. Through this act of violence she has received a wonderful gift. Many women in this very predicament choose to view the situation in a positive light. This baby brings great joy to her life. Again, the power of positive thinking is enormous. If you can find love in a situation, you can view it positively.

If giving birth to this child would cause even greater suffering to this woman, then it can be viewed differently; an abortion in this case is working towards her personal greater good. Free will enables each woman to make the decision for herself. It is a decision that should not be taken lightly—taking the life of a potential human being. Life is most precious. The soul enters the potential child at the very moment of conception. When people try to validate abortion and claim that it is not yet a human being, they are mistaken. It may not be a human being in its fullest sense, but it is a potential human being and it has a soul as much as you have a soul.

You ask about capital punishement. Capital punishment does not work toward the greater good of mankind. All life is precious, even the life of a hardened criminal. No human being has the authority or right to take a human life. What is accomplished? To kill a man because he murdered another makes the executioner a murderer as well. Murder is a solution, produced by a sad, human condition. This condition comes from fear and a lack of love. Murderers have no love in their hearts, only pain and suffering. To eliminate this pain they choose to kill another, but their pain only grows and is magnified. When the murderer experiences his own personal life review at the moment of death he will experience all the suffering inflicted upon his victims. This is not punishment, although it certainly could be interpreted as such. It is a demonstration of all things not good that this man experienced in his life. This demonstration is so that the man can make a choice in his next lifetime to experience all that is good.

You are all on a progression towards the greater good of mankind. You have all experienced that which is not good so that you can fully recognize and appreciate all that is good. You have all suffered in ways that you cannot imagine. It is all part of the process of progression. Pray for the poor souls who are suffering, send them your loving energy. They need your prayer. In time all suffering will cease, it will not be a necessity any longer. All souls on their path of evolution will have learned this great lesson: Killing simply does not work towards the greater good. With pure love in the hearts of many, suffering will slowly, but surely, melt away.

At times God would just speak to me. Not as an answer to a question asked. More like poetry of some sort. I thought these words were beautiful and worthy to be written down and shared. I received the following when I did not have any questions to ask. I asked dear God to communicate with me through words. This is what I got:

Behold! Admire the beauty all around you!
The lonely rose growing in a tangle of weeds.
Sweet fragrance drifts softly on the air,
soft as the skin of a babe,
color of life's blood.
The sun beckons to this rose, pulling it skyward,
radiating its light and love to the rose.
Petals dry and wither, fall gently to the ground,
discarded remnants of the beauty that once was.
In time the rose shrinks and dies.
The seasons change.
Old Man Winter visits the land in a frozen triumph.
Spring joyfully arrives and winter comes to pass.
Bees stir from the ground,
birds return from their long journey,
rivers overflow with their abundance.
The rose is born once again.
It grows tall and beautiful among a sea of like roses.
This beautiful rose stands above the rest.
It is more beautiful, its scent more fragrant.
It knows the Light and Love beckoning to it above.
Every day it reaches towards this Light, growing and changing,
but always moving towards the Light.
It is the perfect rose. It is a rose of Love.
The time comes when the sea of roses
and the perfect rose once more wither and die.
Rebirth is imminent . . . the seasons change once again.
Many roses grow tall with the perfect rose of Love.
Several stand tall above the rest.
Their beauty immeasurable; their Love immense.
They know the sun, they have found joy in their existence.
Many years pass,
the sea of roses are now all standing tall,
every one reaching for the Light and Love of the sun.
It is a glorious day—the sun shines happily,
knowing the Love between sun and rose is everlasting.

Do you have a simple message for my children?

Yes! Dear little children, love your mommy and daddy. They are the only mommy and daddy you have. They love you more than anybody else! Love me, God. I am *your* God, talk to me. I listen to you. I love you just like your mommy and daddy. Be kind to each other. Be kind to all the people you love and all the people you meet. When you are kind you will be very happy in your heart. Do what makes you happy. Find your dreams and follow them. You can be anything you want to be. Do not be afraid to try and keep trying. Remember that I am always here for you. God is everywhere you look. Call on your angels to help you when you feel you are in danger or in trouble. I will send them to you to help you.

Try, *try* harder to be loving to your sister, Jake. Try, *try* harder to be loving to your brother, Marianna. Having a brother or sister is very, very special. You are lucky to have each other. You picked each other to go through your life as brother and sister. You even picked your mommy and daddy. You all wanted to be together. So make the very best of being together. Love each other! Tell every member of your family how much you love them. It makes them feel so happy!

Work hard and play hard. Experience some of both every

day. Remind your mommy and daddy to play, too. At the end of the day rest easy, have sweet, peaceful dreams. Begin the next day fresh. It is a new day, a day when you can start all over. Any mistakes that are made the day before should be forgotten. Try to be good to one another on this new day. Above all, remember your mommy and daddy love you, no matter what you do or say. Even when you are mean and rotten, they still love you. But being mean and rotten does not make you feel very good inside. Being loving and kind is really what feels good. Especially when someone is loving and kind right back. Doesn't it feel great?

I love you, my dear little children. I am God. I am all-powerful. I am all things that are good. I am a great white light of energy, so strong and filled with love. I am all the beautiful things that surround you. The flowers and the trees growing, the big moon in the sky that follows you wherever you go, the birds singing to you. Everything in nature is part of God. You are even part of God. God is *everything good*. Love me, you will feel very good inside when you do.

What is God?

God is the unknown essence. Indescribable is the vastness of God's existence. God is all things. Everything! Look around you, everywhere you will see God. God is in the past, present, and future all at once. God transcends this thing of time. God is a great, all-powerful energy that radiates throughout the entire universe. All the elements are part of God. Every little, tiny piece of *everything* is God, from the smallest, invisible atom to the infinite space of the universe. Everything your senses can perceive is God. You are God! God is a pure, white, blinding light. Every color combined creates this unbelievable light. The power of this light is greater than a trillion suns times a trillion suns. This power, this energy is infinite. It goes on forever. It has always been here. It has no beginning and no end.

This God has the power to create. All creation comes from this God. God is something that cannot be explained with words, or feeling, or intuition alone. God is *all* experience. God is all things hidden, and all things seen. Your connection with this glorious God is of tremendous importance. One cannot deny oneself. Each soul is created with the true nature of God. Each being is pure and holy in its birth. Human souls are of God. They are forever immortal, everlasting and perpetual. The physical world of man is a world of imperfection. God gave each created soul the capacity to know God and to love God. Within this capacity lies perfection! Perfection is eternal! This is the progression of your existence. Divine bounties await you in the kingdom of God. True knowledge is the knowledge of God.

Once a soul has reached a state of pure love, of holy perfection, the gates to the knowledge of God will open wide before your very eyes. This knowledge is the great unknown. It cannot be described in earthly terms. Your physical life shall come to an end. You shall return to God, your home. God has created all, all return to God. Upon this returning, all mysteries will be solved, all questions will be answered. The great unknown will reveal itself. This is a most glorious time for the soul! Pure love abounds. God in the most simplest of terms is this: *Love.*

How can a mother abandon her child?

Very few children are truly abandoned. Most mothers do really love their children. In their hearts they believe that giving the child up is in the best interest of the child. They arrive at this decision with great difficulty. They love their child, but fear they will not be a good mother, that someone else would do better in raising them. They may be right. The life of a child is most precious. Children should be treasured, valued beyond comprehension. Bringing children into the world is something that should not ever be taken lightly. The original reason for procreation was to populate the great Earth with many people. This was accomplished rather quickly, and the sole purpose of procreation evolved and changed. When a man and woman create a family, ideally it should be out of a great love for one another.

The making of a child should not be for personal gain or to try to keep the love of another. Love cannot be captured and held prisoner. True love can only be given freely with no conditions whatsoever.

Some women who bring forth a child do so for all the wrong reasons. They may say it was not their choice. But this is not true. They chose to engage in the act that brought forth the child. The child may have been created "by accident"— but really, was it? There are no accidents. In this regard, the mother made a choice. If she wishes to believe it was accidental, this is certainly what she will believe. When the choice is made to bring forth a child who is really not wanted, something very sad happens. The mother becomes fearful and loses all confidence in raising that child. How can she successfully raise a child whom she does not truly want? She may have chosen to have the child because she fears losing the man she loves. She may have chosen to have the child to draw love and attention to herself. She may have made this choice to possess the life of a child, like so many other possessions.

None of these is a reason to give birth to the precious miracle of a child. Nine months is a sufficient time to prepare for the birth of a child. In preparation, the mother may realize that she has made a mistake. In realizing her error—that a child should not be brought forth for her own personal gain—the mother does one of two things. If she is on the spiritual path to God, she turns inward for strength; she prays for guidance. I hear her prayer. Slowly, as the child grows within her protective womb, her love for the child slowly grows as well. She realizes that this child is wanted. This child is the grandest desire of her heart. She just did not know it. This mother makes the choice to not abandon her child.

Now, the other choice a mother can make is that of true abandonment. The mother disconnects herself from that child. She does not even view herself as mother to this child. She does not experience the love and wonderment that should be experienced at such a miracle. She has already abandoned this child with her heart. This poor child is without a mother. For even if the mother chooses to remain a part of this child's life and chooses to raise this child, she is truly not mother to this child. She may be birth mother, but surely she is not mother in the way that is intended for the greater good of mankind. This sad child grows up not knowing the precious love that exists between mother and child.

If this mother chooses to give this child to another, in so doing she has set herself free from blame. She has relinquished the responsibility of raising this child correctly and with love. This child is better off without this mother. This child will find love in the world on his own. Healing must occur for this child. Some children are never able to heal from true abandonment. They are plagued by it their entire lives. To heal, they must realize that regardless of circumstances their life is most precious. They are a miracle of God. As such, they are made of pure love even if their parent does not want them.

They can grow strong if they make that choice in their life. They can seek out people in their lives who love unconditionally. They can find love through a family of their own. They must be very careful not to make the same mistake their very mother made. Having a child cannot be for ulterior motives.

Ideally, a child is brought into the world when a couple is very deeply in love, committed to each other for life, when they love themselves as individuals worthy of parenthood. They pray for the gift of a child. And when that child arrives, they rejoice and are so grateful for this great gift. They are filled with wonder—how beautiful, how unbelievably precious this life is! You ask why a mother would abandon her child? True abandonment is a result of the great fear of this mother.

She has no confidence in herself, she is absorbed in this fear. She is so desperate to receive love herself. This child cannot provide love to the mother, and the mother cannot provide love for the child unless the mother first loves herself. This mother is part of God. This mother has no love of self. This mother has no love for God. For if she did, she would not be capable of truly abandoning her very own flesh.

When I say "*true* abandonment," I am not referring to the mother who gives her child up out of love because she believes she is looking out for the child's best interest. I am referring to a mother who chooses to leave a child behind, or chooses to abort her child, or chooses to even kill her own child, because she simply does not care. This demonstrates how important the love of God is. With this love anything can be accomplished, even if the mother lacks confidence or experiences fear; if she has a love for God, all things will work out. I call to this mother, I try to speak to her through the beauty all around her. If she would only hear my call, she would feel my love for her, she would experience love of herself, and she would have the capacity to love her child.

My dear mother, Bonnie, had a difficult time growing up. When she was very young, her parents divorced. My grandmother took my mother's older sister Ann with her and left my mother behind with my grandfather. I have come to realize now that she did this because she thought my mother would be happier living with my grandfather. Tragically, my mother lost complete touch with her mother and sister. I asked the question, "How can a mother abandon her child?" with my mother in mind. The answer I got was very insightful, but I felt that so much was missing. I went back to bed that night wondering if God had really given me a full answer. The next morning, I awoke. It happened to be my mom's birthday, June fifth.

I sat in a chair in my living room and read what I had written the night before regarding abandonment.

After I finished reading, I sat for a while pondering what was on the paper. I looked up and saw on my dining room wall a beautiful reflection. It was about three feet high by four inches wide. It was so bright! From the top of the reflection to the middle, there were about ten little shapes, kind of like butterflies. It looked so pretty. It really grabbed my attention. I could not take my eyes away from it.

My four-year-old daughter walked into the room. She looked up at the reflection and asked, "Mommy, what is that?" I told her it was just a reflection coming from somewhere in the room. She asked, "Where?" I looked around the room. I could not find its source. I kept touching different objects in the dining room, thinking that the reflection was coming from there. Then I went into the living room and discovered the source of the reflection. It was the antique mirror hanging on the wall. My grandmother's antique mirror!

With that, I sat back down in the chair. I got an overwhelming feeling that it was my grandmother, Mary. She was sending me a sign. It was almost as if she was saying, "Here I am, I am present in your life, I am sorry for any pain I caused you, I love you." I was absolutely sure she needed to get a message to me to give my mother on her birthday. I went to my computer, turned it on, waited for it to boot up. As I waited, I said a silent prayer to God to let me speak to my grandmother, Mary. The following is what I was able to write:

Bonnie, dear, I did not abandon you! I loved you very, very much. I simply let you go. It was an extremely difficult thing for me to do. I cried many tears because of this. If I knew then how hard it would be for you to grow up without a mother, I don't think I would have reached the same difficult decision. Your father loved you and Ann so very much. He loved me very much. And when we parted as husband and wife, I still did love him in many, many ways, deep down inside. But I also feared and hated him as well.

There was a side to him you never knew. I am glad you did not ever have to encounter his dark side. He was (and is!) a wonderful, wonderful soul, regardless of our differences. We knew that we would divorce. It just could not be worked out. He wanted you and Ann. I wanted you and Ann. I could not imagine us working things out, at the time, nor did I want to. We should have tried harder. We should have tried for our children's sake. Today it is much easier for a couple to divorce and still have a relationship. It was not so in our time, in our case.

You were so young and precious. You loved your father more than you loved me at that time in your life. You both absolutely adored one another. He adored Ann as well, but you were his little one. I knew that he could never, ever harm you. That he would always love and take care of you. I knew that I could not take you from him. I also knew that he would not be able to go on living if I took both you and Ann from him. I could not bear this decision. But the decision was made for me. I felt in my heart it was the right thing to do. I must tell you it was the hardest thing I ever did. I am not asking you for any sort of sympathy. I made this decision and I will forever live with it. I am asking you for your forgiveness. I know it brought you great pain. You never got over it. I so want your heart to heal. When I made a new life for myself with your sister Ann, I tried hard to forget you. Not because I didn't love you but because I did love you. I never, ever forgot you.

I kept some of your things with me, and whenever I moved they went with me, for many, many years. At some point I lost track of these few items. One was a lock of your blond hair. Another was a small doll you loved as a baby. It was your lovey. It reminded me so much of you. As the years went by I did not look for you. I was so afraid. Please, please forgive me for not looking for you. I should have. I was so afraid of seeing you again and I wanted so badly to see you again. When we did finally meet again, you were a grown woman. You did not need me to try to be mother to you at that point. You were hurt and angry. But you tried to be cordial. Thank you for trying. We missed much in life together as mother and daughter.

I want you to know that in this afterlife existence I have tried to help you. My presence is with you. When you went through your surgery, you needed my loving touch. I was there. Did you feel me? I can never make up to you the great hurt you have experienced. I am your mother. The only mother you have ever had. It is sad that your image of me is something I do not want you to remember. Please, please remember the loving moments we did experience together. We had many of them. You were young, but if you try hard you can remember them.

Remember the golden, gay times we spent together as a family? It was so beautiful at the beach. I can remember you playing in the sand with your yellow bucket and blue shovel as if it were yesterday. I think there was a duck on it? I can remember your father going into the ocean with Ann. Coming out of the water so strong and handsome. Know that we have forgiven each other in the afterlife. There is only love and forgiveness in this place of Heaven. We are both at great peace. Call on both of us when you need us. We are forever a part of your life. If you wish us to make our presence known, just ask us. I love you, my dear Bonnie. Happy birthday.

Lovingly,
Your mother Mary

My greatest wish is that this message brings peace to my beloved mother. I truly feel that it was brought to me specifically on her birthday this year because she was ready to hear this message from her mother. Every question I have asked of God has gently led me to the next question. Often I had no idea where these questions were going to take me next. Through each answer I have gained infinite wisdom, and light in my life.

What has made me happiest is that I have been able to provide light and love to other lives as well. Especially to those whom I hold dearest in my heart. I sincerely hope to be able to progress in my ability to help others with information I can bring to them from the spiritual world. This is my greatest desire! If I can accomplish this in my present lifetime, I will be infinitely blessed. God keeps telling me that "you create whatsoever you desire." Surely, God speaks the truth.

What about good versus evil?

My child, these dualities are the basic building blocks of the universe. In every single human experience there is a complete opposite in operation. This is the ultimate complexity and simplicity of universal law. I have spoken of this before. The yin, the yang; the alpha, the omega; the good, the evil; the positive, the negative. In order for so much good to exist, the bad—"evil"—must coexist. It is a necessity in the world as you know it. There's always a balance of good and evil in effect. Whether good is greater or less than evil at any given time, or evil is greater or less than good at any given time, does not matter; the balance is always in effect. The dualities are always present. The equilibrium maintains.

I am your God. In the physical world I experience *all* things through my children, whom I created to do just that— to experience all there is. I live vicariously through each and every one of you. This is why I love each and every one of you—the sinner, the saint. God's love of self is everlasting and does not ever falter. In the kingdom of Heaven, evil does not have a need to exist. This is difficult to reiterate. But the physical world and the spiritual world are different in many, many ways. The great mysteries that await you are so wondrous. But for now we are talking of the physical world in which you exist presently.

The evil that exists in man's heart is such, so that all things good may also exist. You can see this demonstrated in the most profound ways. When a great tragedy occurs to one individual, many gather to uplift and help the family. The positive energy flows freely back to those who need it most. These people arise above the great tragedy that has occurred in their lives. They are compassionate and loving to one another. They support each other in this tremendous time of need. The way humans go through a bereavement process is extraordinary. The whole process is designed to bring out the positive aspects of human nature. You ask, "What can I do to help those who have suffered this tragedy?" You would do anything to help them. You bring flowers, food, your love-energy, beautiful words to inspire, your prayers—all this arises from the tragedy that occurred. This process is very important and it demonstrates to you how the positive arises from the negative. Think about it. All negative actions inspire positive reactions.

Human beings have wasted so many of the Earth's great gifts. Forests have been destroyed. Animal species have been wiped out. The waters have been polluted. The very soil has been exhausted. The great Earth's protective layer has been damaged by the abuses of mankind. Yet because mankind has realized what it has done, positive energy is beginning to flow back into the great Earth. Slowly, slowly it will be repaired, because this will become the desire of the great masses of people. The positive will arise from the negative. Ways and means will continually be discovered so that the precious Earth may heal and be well once again. Negative experience must exist so that positive experience may respond to the negative. Much of the negativity does not have the positive response that is necessary. When this occurs the negative energy builds and builds. It must be released in little bursts. These bursts are where all catastrophic events come from. Earthquake, flood, hurricane, tornado, disease, famine—all forms of mass destruction. These all arise out of a buildup of unbelievable, enormous negative energy.

After a great storm in which mass destruction has taken place, one finds that the sun comes out; often a rainbow appears as inspiration to the people. Many people gather. They rub their eyes and blink. They are amazed at the wreckage around them. They mourn their loss. But they very rapidly take positive action. They immediately thank God for their lives. They begin to help one another with enormous positive love-energy. They rebuild, they assist, they feed the hungry and shelter those who seek shelter. Many others come to their aid in this time of need. Lives are often sacrificed for the greater good of the many.

Those who remain in this physical world are forever changed by their experience. Whenever human beings endure great tragedy of any kind in their lives, either they emerge from it stronger than ever before or they die inside. This is their choice. If they have a connection with the divine source of love, God, they emerge stronger. If they open their hearts, I fill them with love. They only need to open up to this divine source and love will pour forth if that is their desire. So often a person who has endured suffering has been asked, "How did you get through it?" The answer is always, "God got me through. My faith and the love of God got me through it."

What is faith?

In trying to explain faith, I must tell you that hope is of utmost importance in regard to faith. Faith is knowing in your heart that no matter what you endure, with the love of God and this connection with the divine source of love, you may endure all that you encounter in this life of yours. Faith is when all doubt vanishes. You trust that God will provide. You trust that you already have been provided for. You trust that you have the capacity for all things good within yourself. You trust that you are a mere human being who often makes mistakes, but tries to right the wrongs. When you have faith in all these things, you cannot help but have a great hope for everything.

Faith in God brings hope to those who seek it. No matter what tragedy befalls those with faith, they remain hopeful. Hopeful that tomorrow will be a better day. These joyful souls know the greatest secret: there is life everlasting with God. They do not question it. They know above all things, through their faith, that God exists. God has always existed, and God is of paramount importance in their lives. Those of little faith go through their lives with so much doubt. Doubt about themselves, doubt about the world operating around them, doubt of eternal life, doubt of love, doubt of a God.

Let me tell you, those with faith can do great things,

because they do not waste their time worrying and doubting the existence of a great universal force operating, of which they are all a part. Those with faith have already accomplished great things in their lives. They are only to succeed. Because even through their mistakes, even through their losses, they have faith and they have hope. Even if their entire physical life is that of constant struggle, those with faith know that in the afterlife, the struggle will be nevermore. A paradise awaits them.

Those with faith know this, they do not question it. For some, faith comes and goes, like the beautiful moon, waxing and waning at different times in their lives. But if they stop and take notice, when their faith is strongest, when their moon/faith is full, everything becomes illuminated. Everything is basking in the light of a love so strong and brilliant.

Remember your deepest feeling when you have this great faith and overwhelming hope in your heart. I promise you, my dear children, that a profoundly wondrous existence awaits you in the afterlife. My children with faith already know this, they do not need my promise, they do not need my words to tell them this. They already know it in their hearts. They do not question it. Have faith, dear ones. Through this faith, hope will arise. When you live your life with hope in your heart, faith is always there. It is a wonderful circle of faith and hope, both connected, both everlasting, flowing from one to the other. Have faith, dear ones.

How important is charity?

Charity is a key factor in man's progression towards the greater good. Power and greed are sought by the many. This great search causes many of your problems. Ambition is one thing, greed is another. Those with greed in their hearts do not hesitate to hurt another while in the process of acquiring their riches. Most crime is committed from either greed or poverty. Those who are greedy want more money, they want more power over others. Through their business dealings they are unscrupulous. They get richer and richer, but they never have enough money, enough possessions, or enough happiness in their lives.

Those who live in a state of utter poverty need money to survive, yet they have so little. They cannot provide for even the most basic necessities such as food and shelter. In this state of desperation, it is not unusual for them to steal from another. They are merely trying to survive.

These states of extreme wealth and extreme poverty are not good. There is no balance. Charity is necessary. If only those with so much would help those with so little. Many wealthy people do just that. They give millions of dollars away to charitable organizations. These organizations are a wonderful idea. They are doing some good in this world. But it is the individual who still suffers greatly. There is a silly modern American saying that goes something like, "He who dies with the most toys, wins." When you pass from this world to the next, upon your life review, you will not remember the many toys and possessions you had in your life. What you will remember are the many lives you touched. You will experience in an instant the profound connections you made with those encountered in your life. The saying should be, "He who dies with the most friends, wins." I like this much more. Don't you?

Charity towards your fellow man is of utmost importance. Your souls will not progress fully until the world operates in a state of charity. When the great masses of people have love in their hearts, charity will be inevitable. People will begin to give each other the "shirts off their backs." They will not need so many possessions. With pure love within, the great hole will be filled.

Many people living in this present world try to fill this hole with money. Someday, when mankind is truly ready for its progression to accelerate, extremes of wealth and poverty will cease to exist. A system will be implemented by a world government in which everyone will work at doing what they love. Everyone will have a job. Every single person will perform some sort of activity that provides for the welfare of all. There will be no money. That's right! No money. This is hard for you to believe—a world without money. I am giving you mere glimpses of what the distant future holds. Remember, time is a great circle. In Heaven there is no time. Every moment is in the now. God is aware of all moments in time at once. This does not mean that everything is predetermined. It is not. Man has free will to alter the way things happen and how rapidly they happen as well. But ultimately the end result will be the same.

Mankind in time will be operating in a manner in which every single individual is working towards the greater good of all humanity. Each individual will live a life of love. Every action in their lives will work towards this state of pure love. People will work to provide for each other, rather than for themselves as individuals. No one will be extremely wealthy, and no one will be extremely poor. Every person will live comfortably, yet simply. Industry will strive to heal the great Mother Earth. When the quest for money does not exist, your sole purpose in your life's work will totally change. Your purpose will be to strive toward the greater good. There will be no reason to steal from another. Everyone will have their needs met. There will be no more competition. Instead, there will be cooperation. Cooperation at all levels of the economy and of the social order.

The more the world aspires towards the greater good, the more that cooperation will be ever-present. Mutual aid and helpfulness will abound. Man's very nature will be altered forever. There will be a fair and just distribution of goods and services. The human, natural, and material resources at our disposal will be used for the long-term good of all the people, not the short-term profit of the few who are wealthy. All will be working together towards the same goal. All will be working towards the greater good. All talents will be utilized. People will all have the same educational opportunities. This is a vital part of being able to do what you love doing. Unbelievable technological advancements will take place at this time. People will not waste so much energy trying to acquire wealth. Individuals, in doing what they love, will be able to experience immense creativity, great fulfillment, and ultimate spiritual advancement.

> *On this day I received yet another of God's beautiful messages to me:*

God is always with you. I am with you through your joy, your laughter; I am with you through your sorrow, your tears. I am with you in your struggle, your pleasure, your pain. I am with you in health, I am with you in sickness. At your beautiful conception I am present, as I am with you in your death of body. Your eternal soul knows my presence. This soul will always return home to me, your God. In this physical life of yours you sense my presence. . . . I speak softly to you. Listen for my voice. It may come to you in many different forms, but all these forms are my true essence. I am forever present with you, my dear children. Know me, recognize me, connect with me, trust in me, have faith in me, have hope through me. I am your God and I love you eternally.

Cloning—is this a bad thing?

It is not for God to say if this is good or bad for mankind. Remember, I do not make judgments regarding "right" or "wrong." I can say that this development in scientific advancement is going to be very controversial. With the cloning of humans, the end of all disease is a possibility, but—this is a very delicate matter. Cloning cannot be used for the greater good and the advancement of the species toward all things good until the great masses of people are ready to use it for these purposes. This is the very reason that it will raise such controversy. There will be many doctors and scientists trying to clone human beings for reasons that do not raise the species to the next level, towards the greater good. This will cause a lot of problems; it will take many years for the debate to be finally settled. Mankind is not quite ready to take on this great cloning experiment. Hopefully, the great masses will have this wisdom and realize it is not yet time. If cloning is used when people are ready to use it for the greater good, then it will be used in a very positive way. Beware of those who are not planning to use it for the greater good. This could be a dangerous thing.

You wonder if the cloned human will have the same soul as the first. No, he will not. It is not possible to replicate a human soul, or any soul, for that matter. Each soul is unique. Each soul has its own agenda, its own rate of progress. Each soul has its own individual personality. This personality can slowly change over time, but basically it remains with the soul for its entire existence, from lifetime to lifetime. Once a soul is brought forth, it lives eternally. When a human being is cloned, a new soul will enter the cloned shell of the body. These two humans of flesh will share almost every characteristic. They will have the same DNA. They will have the same level of intelligence. Their personalities will be very similar. But their souls could be as different as night and day. It cannot be determined what type of soul would choose to experience life in the body of a cloned human being.

If Hitler were cloned, it is possible that his clone could have a soul that was near pure love, working towards the greater good. This other Hitler would be very different indeed. Body and mind do have free will on the earth plane. This free will can often conflict with the desires of the soul. But the soul is ever-present, it is that small voice inside you— your conscience, your higher self.

If you pay attention to that voice, if you connect with your higher self, that is your choice. Not all choose to make the connection. If you are connected with the great force of God, with this incredibly powerful love, you are very in tune and aware of the desires of your soul. Unfortunately, there are many people walking around who do not make this connection with their soul. They have forgotten their true mission on Earth. They have not been able to remember their truest mission.

There are many variables that can affect the outcome of this cloning you speak of. That is why it must be handled with the utmost care. If cloning is used before the great masses of people exist in a state of pure love, anything is possible. The closer mankind is to the greater good, the closer they are to an existence of pure love. Then it is inevitable that cloning will be used in a positive manner.

The further mankind is from this greater good I keep referring to, the more likely it is that cloning will be used in a destructive manner. I want to stress the importance of being in touch with your soul. All souls are on the path towards the greater good. If the original human being remembered this in his physical existence, that would be a good thing. If the cloned human being remembered his soul's desire, that also would be a good thing. All souls progress at different rates, and are on different levels in their evolution. Where the original human being is in regard to its spiritual path, and where the cloned human being is in regard to his path, can be very different, or very similar. Anything is possible, everything is possible. It depends on what the desires of the great masses of people are at any given moment in time on the physical plane of Earth. Great shifts will take place slowly over time with regard to this desire.

My religious instruction was limited. I attended church on and off over the years. I have always been searching for my own answers, my own truths. My own personal beliefs regarding God are based more on spirituality than religion. Regardless of this, my family celebrates all the Christian holidays and I embrace Christ as being a very important prophet of God. Some of my questions are regarding Christ, because this is my background. This is what I know. But I embrace many other diverse beliefs as well. It is in the acceptance and appreciation of this diversity that we may have unity of mankind, all working towards the greater good.

Will there be a second coming of Christ?

Yes. Christ will come again, in the not too distant future, but not in this lifetime that you are living. Remember, Jesus Christ was able to reach a state of pure love. Christ did perform great miracles because of this. He had the power to heal. He had the power to defy the physical limitations of his own flesh. He inspired many others with his love. Christ became an icon, representing the power of God's love. God and love are one and the same. These words can be used interchangeably. Christ left behind a legacy of this love, as did other prophets. This legacy has been passed on from generation to generation.

In many ways, Christ was an ordinary man. Yet he reached a level of spiritual evolution so high that he created Heaven on Earth for himself. His complete being and essence was one of pure love. With this absolute, pure love, all things are possible.

There are humans doing work right now in this present earthly existence—performing miracles of the soul, miracles of God. These individuals are very close to existing in that state of pure love I speak of. Very close, but not quite there yet. The closer one gets, the more miraculous their existence becomes. The soul and God are one. You are all pieces of God—little, tiny pieces that make up the great sum of God.

Every little piece of God has it within itself to exist in a state of pure love on the physical earth plane. This is usually a long and difficult journey for each individual soul. Few souls have actually been able to accomplish this. Christ is one of these souls. Christ will choose to come again. He will incarnate into human flesh again. He will walk among you. He will be flesh of your flesh. When he incarnates into this physical world he will forget that he is Christ. But remember, this Christ child of God has achieved pure love. Once you have achieved this state, you do not regress. You will always be that of pure love, forevermore.

This new Christ will not make claim to being Christ of old and will not remember that he or she was the Christ of old. The subconscious soul will always remember this. But it is lost by the human, physical experience. Glimpses of this memory will surface into the conscious mind. This new Christ will inspire new thought, new advancement in the spiritual growth of the world. This new Christ may go by another name. The messages brought forth will be very important in the Earth's advancement and its very survival.

The world is going to undergo great changes. There will be struggle and strife before a new world emerges. Do not waste your time and energy worrying about the inevitability of these occurrences. It is all part of the progression. It is necessary. Trust that all will work out, over many thousands of years. God has always existed, God brought forth the wondrous souls who inhabit the Earth. These souls are all pieces of God; they will exist forever, for all eternity, just as God exists eternally.

These souls are able to change their form in the physical world, in the physical dimensions they choose to inhabit. They can be created in the physical world. In time they deteriorate, their physical form changes and eventually withers and dies. But this is only their physical existence. The soul's existence is perpetual, unending. It has the capacity to change its physical form in any way it chooses.

There are many physical forms it can take on. You have not even discovered all these forms as of yet! The soul has the great power of pure love within. Each soul has this great power. Christ was able to realize this great power here, on the earth plane. Christ will choose to come again. You ask when, when will Christ come again? He will come when he is needed.

Christ achieved pure love. My child—do you know what is the simplest and yet most powerful action which can bring you closer to this pure love?

A smile.

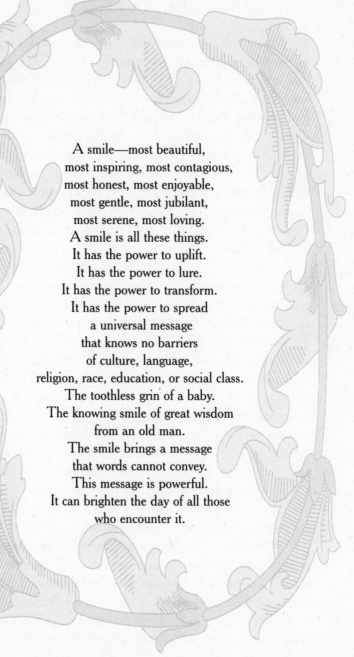

A smile—most beautiful,
most inspiring, most contagious,
most honest, most enjoyable,
most gentle, most jubilant,
most serene, most loving.
A smile is all these things.
It has the power to uplift.
It has the power to lure.
It has the power to transform.
It has the power to spread
a universal message
that knows no barriers
of culture, language,
religion, race, education, or social class.
The toothless grin of a baby.
The knowing smile of great wisdom
from an old man.
The smile brings a message
that words cannot convey.
This message is powerful.
It can brighten the day of all those
who encounter it.

How do our dreams and nightmares relate to our lives?

Night dreams are important. The source of these dreams is your mind working on a subconscious level. This is the level that recognizes your soul. It is also the level that remembers your truest mission on this Earth in your physical life. Some of the recurring dreams you have personally experienced over many, many years reflect past life experiences that you are catching mere glimpses of. In these recurring dreams, you visit locations that feel so comfortable to you. As if you have been there many times before. You have! Not all people experience their dreams in such a revealing way. Many people do not even think they dream. All have night dreams. It is just that not all remember them.

In your dreams you can experience things that you cannot necessarily experience in your lifetime. You may receive prophetic dreams of a future unfolding. You do not even realize that they are prophetic in nature. In fact, you find them startling or weird. The future holds unexplainable wonders. Some of your dreams have hidden meaning. If you can decipher a dream's meaning, you will find it very beneficial. Think of the characters and events in your dreams as symbols of what is happening to you in your life at the given moment. If you examine them very closely, you will find that there may be a hidden message telling you how to solve the problems in your everyday life. The nightmares you experience are your most powerful and frightening dreams. They are very necessary.

I have spoken to you about the need to experience all things not good so that you may recognize and appreciate all that is good. Through your nightmares you are able to experience "virtual not-good." These not-good, terrifying nightmares that you experience are truly real for you. You have done such a good job in creating them for yourself that you are able to understand, recognize, and appreciate the things that are good in your life. The nightmares you have are all about that which you fear most.

You have experienced this fear in a very real way. It is not necessary for it to manifest itself. You do not dwell on it, and this is a good thing. You never want to dwell on something that is negative. You never want to give it too much of your energy. If you give it your energy, it is possible that it will be created.

So when you encounter the negative in your dreams as well as in your life, experience it for what it is and then quickly let it go. Do not allow yourself to waste your time with such negativity. Fill your very being with great love-energy. Connect with the divine source of God's unending love. Be positive in your words, in your thinking, and in your actions.

I have always felt that the opportunities that have come my way have not just been by chance.

What is the role of mysterious coincidences in our lives?

Your opportunities have not come your way by chance. These opportunities were created by *you*. You are responsible for your own success and your own happiness. No one else is. You cannot be responsible for someone else's happiness, either. If you think about the path your life has taken, you will remember many times when things magically worked out for you. Is it not amazing the magic that you are capable of creating? You could be minding your own business, going through your busy day when a chance encounter occurs with someone, be it a stranger or long-lost friend.

If you take the time to talk to this person, you will often find he or she has just the message, just the information that you were looking for. Many of your experiences in your life have led you to the now. To the present moment. Everything you have learned, everything you have experienced has significant relevance to what you are trying to accomplish in this life.

If you are on the spiritual path and have made the connection with God, then you will find out what you set out to accomplish in the first place. Remember, you chose the circumstances of your birth—the who, where, and what—so that you could accomplish something in this life. Whatever your mission is, it relates to moving toward the greater good of all mankind.

If you take a step back and look at how you happened to find your friends, your career, your spouse, your possessions (car, house, et cetera), you will see a mysterious pattern of events that seemed coincidental. Things just worked out so perfectly! One door closed and another opened. This happens again and again. Act on the potential opportunities coming your way. Explore the possible messages coming to you from so many sources. You need to be alert. You have to slow down to do this. You have to take the time to meet and greet all the people you encounter. You never know what message they may have for you.

If you are not friendly, if you do not speak to them, you will never know what the message is. If you have an open mind and an open heart, you will find that the information you are seeking will arrive just as you need it. This principle works with receiving information, but it also works with whatever it is you are seeking, be it a new friend with whom you can share a common passion, or some object of your desire (new couch, the perfect necklace, the exact shade of purple dress to match your new necklace, and so on), a doctor to treat whatever ails you, a solution to any trivial problem you encounter.

Your intuition can help guide you to make the right connections to create whatsoever you desire. These "coincidences" are not merely what they seem. They are very intentional, deliberate ways of getting exactly what you want from life. In getting what you want, do not forget to uplift those who bring you these messages. It is very important that you give as well as receive. In giving, you will receive. Send your loving energy to the people you meet along the way. Uplift them to a higher level. In uplifting them, you will raise yourself to a new level. Stay alert; focus. Pay attention to these not-so-mysterious events that guide you toward your original mission.

How important is our intuition?

God has provided you with six senses. You see all the beauty before you with your eyes: the rainbow in the sky after a powerful storm, the sun rising and setting in the sky, the great Earth and all its splendor. You perceive sound with utmost clarity with your ears: the cry of your baby awakening from slumber, the wonderful music that invigorates your soul, the car approaching you while you ride your bike.

You taste and smell that which is bitter and that which is sweet. How sweet the smell of a rose. How unique and wonderful the response you have when you bite into a wedge of lime! Your sense of touch can tell you about the world in profound ways, through your hands you can work magic. By your touch you can heal, you can create, you can write the very words on this page! And this wonderful sense of touch is not limited to your hands. Your entire body can perceive this touch!

Now you have another sense. A sense that is just as integral to your life's experience as the ones just mentioned. But this sense is unheard and unseen. It is not from your physical or mental states of being. It is part of your emotional state of being. This sense is derived not from your body, nor from your mind. It is derived from your soul. This sense is your intuition.

It is an integral part of your human existence. Your mental, emotional, and physical processes are all affected by this intuition I speak of. Just as you were born with all your senses, your intuition is present as well. Each and every moment, you receive information intuitively. You are just not always aware of the process. If you can become aware of the unconscious information your intuition brings to you, you can integrate this information into your conscious experience.

Some people are able to truly connect with their intuitive sense. This is a great gift. But all people have the potential to use this gift. It is an integral part of each and every one of God's children. All these senses were given to you as wondrous gifts so that you may experience life in all its glory. Your sense of intuition is just as important as your sense of sight. Through this sense you can see the unseen.

Pay attention to the little voice inside your head. Often it provides you with information that you could not know through any of your other senses. Intuition is expressed to you in a language that does not necessarily use words. Intuition is often expressed to you in a feeling, which is an abstract form. You often dismiss these feelings. Do not dismiss them so easily. They are important. These feelings guide you safely through your day-to-day routines. These feelings deliver you from evil. When I speak of evil, I am referring to that which is not good.

Everything you notice has relevance and significance. There is a reason you notice certain things. Pay attention to all you notice. There is hidden information coming to you. Information that can guide you on the path of your life's mission. Information that can answer the questions, Why am I here? What am I to do?

The meaningful coincidences in your life are not nearly as mysterious as they seem. These coincidences are brought to you by way of your intuitive sense. You are interpreting information received by this sense constantly. You do not recognize this. It is as effortless as breathing. You are not aware of every breath you take. Through your intuition you can answer the questions that lie within. Questions that only you hold the answers to.

It has been seven days since I last asked God any questions. I have felt his loving presence in my life continuously. It is truly a blessing to feel this way—especially when you are far away from home. I just returned from a four-day trip to Las Vegas. It was a mixture of business and pleasure. It was my first trip there; it was also my first trip away from my husband and two children. I have never gone away from my kids for more than seven (or so) hours at a time. I was happy to get away for a few days. I think I was finally ready to go somewhere without them. Normally I would be so worried about it that it would not be worth the stress I experience.

My wonderful communication with God has made me confident that everything will be okay when I go away. My plane is not going to crash. No harm will come to my children. My house will not burn to the ground while I am gone. These are worries that would have plagued me to no end just a few short months ago. I have experienced a feeling of serenity that I never could have experienced before. Thank you, God, for this!

I had a wonderfully hectic good time on my trip. By the last day I was glad to be going home. I began missing my family. I remember now that before I left for my trip, my sister Nicole said to me, "It's good for you to get away, it makes you appreciate everything that you have." This comment struck me as kind of amusing. I am one of those people who never needs to go away to realize all that I've got. I realize it each and every day of my life. I am in complete awe and wonder with all of the many gifts and blessings I have in my life. I am so grateful. I do not need to go away to realize this. I always realize this.

My sister's comment started me thinking about other people's perspectives, and how people in general feel about their day-to-day existence. Are they happy? Do they realize they have so much? Why is it that people always want more? Which brings me to my next question:

Why are some people never satisfied?

A sense of satisfaction, like all things, comes from within. All people can be satisfied, no matter what their circumstance. It all depends on the point of view of the individual. How they choose to perceive things is their own doing. Do you see the glass as being half-full or half-empty? There are some people who walk the Earth who will *never* be satisfied, no matter what. This is their own choice. They do not want to be satisfied. They certainly make the people who love them crazy. No matter how hard you try to please someone like this, their happiness is fleeting. They are always in pursuit of some new thing to make them happy. As soon as they receive whatever it is they desired, they want something else. These poor individuals appear to be unbelievably selfish. They are actually "self-less." They do not have a sense for their *true self*. They are so caught up in the existence of their physical self that they have almost completely lost touch with their spiritual "soul" self. This demonstrates how important it is to sense and acknowledge your spiritual nature.

When you truly connect with this aspect of your being, your sense of satisfaction is ever-present. As soon as you disconnect with your soul, there is disharmony. Things just do not feel right. You may not even know what is bothering you. This adds to your frustration, your lack of satisfaction. Let me tell you this: Every person, every individual's life, can boil down to one simple question. Your life is the living of that question, the search for the answer.

First you need to remember what that big question is. In remembering the question, you are then able to begin the work in answering it. All "big" questions lead towards the greater good. They all have the sole purpose of bringing you nearer to the perfect existence of pure love that God is. This all relates to your sense of satisfaction. People who do not possess this satisfaction that I speak of have not discovered what their "big" question is. They have not been able to remember it. This is an extremely frustrating thing. They cannot even begin to work toward answering their question. This work is extremely difficult. And they cannot even begin this difficult work, because they do not even know what question they are trying to answer. You are all born with this question. You all forget this question.

Some people are able to remember their life purpose, their question, early on in their physical existence. This is a wonderful thing. They have a bit of a head start over others. Some people do not remember their life question until they are dying, or even until they have passed on into the next life. All things are realized in the next life/afterlife/Heaven you speak of. How silly it is that you did not make any progress in answering your question. Your entire reason for incarnating into a body, to experience life physically, is an attempt to answer your "big" question.

You will never have a deep sense of satisfaction until you discover what your question is. In just trying to answer your question, you will find complete satisfaction. "Satisfaction guaranteed!" I am not telling you that you will definitely find the answer. The answer will actually bring you something much greater than satisfaction. The mere question will bring you to a place that is mentally, emotionally, and spiritually satisfying. The answer to your question will bring you Heaven on Earth.

>*Dear God, I just want to clarify this. I feel satis-*
>*fied a good amount of the time. I like to think that I*
>*am in touch with my spiritual side a good amount of*
>*the time. But I do not think I have yet discovered my*
>*"big" question. How can I discover it? Have I dis-*
>*covered it and don't know it? Is this possible? Once I*
>*discover it, will I always feel that I am satisfied?*

What is my big question?

So many questions, my dear one. Yes, you do feel satisfied a good amount of the time. This is relative to your being in touch with your spiritual essence, your highest state of being. As I mentioned, when this connection is present you will feel like you are in a tranquil, uplifting "place," no matter what circumstance comes your way. Keep the connection! Try to make that connection when you feel yourself floundering. You can get this feeling of satisfaction back if you try to. Connect with the divine source of love that I am always, *always* sending out to you. This connection can alter your perception of how things are going for you, how satisfied you feel in relationship to your existence.

Your big question is revealing itself to you *right now*, through the writing of this book. When it is complete you will know what your question is. You are very near, it is only a matter of time. It is through the asking of your many questions to me, your God, that you will discover what your life's purpose is. This book is a very important undertaking. It is enabling you to find out your life's question. This is your mission. This is your truest purpose. In your question, you will help many others to discover for themselves what their questions are. Your grandest wishes and desires will be realized, because you have the desire and the power within yourself that they may be realized.

Once your question is discovered, if you remain connected

with the divine source of love, your sense of satisfaction in all things will remain with you always. If you lose your connection, it will feel different to you. You must be conscious of what it feels like when this connection has been broken. If you are conscious of what it feels like, you will be able to recognize and change it. Transform your feelings to those of love; transform your negative thoughts to positive thoughts. The power of this thinking, this "be"-ing, is enormous.

When you begin to realize this power, you will at first be skeptical that it is really so, that this power is so enormous. When you begin to live this way, connected all the time, you will find that it is possible to be satisfied all the time. Satisfied with your physical existence of life on Earth. Satisfied that you are working toward your greater truth. This greater truth of yours, of the individual, is part of the greater truth of all humanity. When all are working toward answering their questions, we will not have discord or dissatisfaction with the ways of the world. We will all truly find happiness. It must begin with the individual. The power to do this great thing lies within each and every one of you reading this right now.

God, you truly inspire and move me. Thank you!
How will I know when my big question is discovered?
How will I know when my book is complete?

Your question will not be revealed until this book is nearly complete. That is the whole purpose of it. When you have realized its purpose, your question will be revealed to you. With this revelation realized, your book will be complete, and you will simply know it.

How can others ask questions of you and also receive answers?

This is a good question. As I have told you before, I hear and listen to every prayer. I speak to every child of mine in different ways. Ways with which they are comfortable. To "speak" to them in words, I have spoken through many prophets. All these prophets brought messages forth that were of utmost importance. They were relevant to the time in which the messages came forth. These messages were always given in a context that could be understood with little difficulty.

Often the messages were distorted as they passed from mouth to ear over hundreds and thousands of years. The messages are not meant to be taken in their literal context. Even when I spoke them originally it was understood that they were metaphors—used because words are insufficient to convey what I want to say to my children. I cannot with words, action, or feeling alone provide you with an understanding of my true essence. It is not something that can be understood. I am the great unknown. Trust me that you will understand in the afterlife what I simply cannot explain to you in this physical life.

Even now as I answer your questions, I am answering them in a manner that you can understand, in a manner that many people in your time will be able to understand. I will speak to many people who wish to communicate with me. The biggest factor in getting this to happen is trusting that it will. Faith can move mountains. Faith can certainly enable you to speak with me. Desire is another huge factor. Your desire to speak with me must be overwhelming. Whatsoever you truly desire is yours. You must maintain hope at all times that I *will* speak with you.

You must have love in your heart as well. Love yourself, love your children, love your spouse, love your neighbor, love your extended family, love your friends, and love all the people that you encounter. Send your loving energy to them. Spread this love wherever you go. Aspire to let no one ever come to you without leaving feeling better and happier. This is a high aspiration. I am not requiring you to live it all the time. I am only asking that you try. The rewards will be substantial. Once you have faith that you can and will speak with me—when you have a strong desire for this communication along with the hope that it will occur, and love in your heart towards yourself and everyone else—then you are ready.

This readiness is imperative for our communication. You are nearly there. The next thing you must do is to settle your mind and body. There are many ways to do this. Each person has his own unique way. Call it meditation, if you want. You need to be completely relaxed in body and mind. You need to slow your breathing. Concentrate on something beautiful near you. See the beauty, feel the beauty.

If you cannot see something beautiful, imagine something beautiful. Take this quiet time to hear the silence. For in this silence, you will hear me. A soft whisper, in the beginning unintelligible. Over time this whisper will form words either on paper or in your mind. Whichever is comfortable to you. You may ask me questions if you wish. I will answer them. You may ask me for guidance if you wish, I will provide you with this guidance. You may ask me for strength, I will give you strength. Talk to me, every day. I hear you. I listen to your every word. If you take the steps that I have just told you, then you will be able to hear my voice speaking to you. It may take a long time for you to experience this communication for yourself. But if you have faith, desire, hope, and love, you have the key elements necessary for the communication. The rest often requires practice.

Learn to quiet yourself. Let the thoughts of your busy day, your family, your business, your worries and problems, let them all fade away as you make your body heavy and still. Relax every muscle from your head down to your toes. Then ask me for the communication. When you communicate with the highest power, that of God, you will feel only love, tremendous joy, and ultimate peace. If you feel anything other than these qualities, you are not having a communication with me. If you encounter a lesser spirit, do not fear it. Ask it to leave you. It will always abide by your will. Ask to communicate only with the highest power. I will affirm this to you when I speak with you.

Just as I told my dear child Yvonne, "You shall find the

answers through me. For I am your God." You will know that it is me. You will know by the way you feel inside. You will experience a peacefulness never experienced before. This wonderful feeling will fill you and overflow. After we have had a communication, this good feeling will remain with you for quite a while. Often it lingers until we speak again to one another. Keep returning to our conversation, because only goodness can come from it.

Tell others; spread the word that anyone can speak to God. The steps are as simple and as complex as they seem to be. Remember faith, desire, hope, and love—anyone can do the rest. The meditation part is the easy part. Anyone can learn to meditate. Read a book, take a class, whatever helps you to learn this skill. It will benefit you in ways too numerous to mention. In this meditative state you will be quiet enough to hear me.

I have finally gotten my children to sleep tonight. Some days I feel like a broken record. Saying the same things to them day in and day out, every day. Despite my scolding, they always know how much I love them.

I love you, my children. . . .

Pick up your toys. Please, don't hit your sister. Brush your teeth—now! Go back to bed. Are you hungry? Don't eat that before dinner. I love you. Take a jacket, it might get cold. Clean up this mess. Do your homework. Get off the phone. Not now, I'm talking. Where are your shoes? I love you. Turn it down. Come over here now. Listen to me. Did you brush your teeth? Go outside and play. Let me kiss it. Give me a hug. I love you. Is your seat belt on? Be quiet now. We'll see. Feed the dog. Feed the cat. Feed the fish. I love you. I'm going to count to three. One. Two. Two and a half . . . Flush the toilet. Who ate all the cookies? I love you. Button your jacket.

Take an umbrella. Your gloves are on the bottom shelf of the closet. I love you. Go to sleep. Do you know what time it is? Let's read a book together. I will help you. You can do it. I love you. Wait your turn. Shut the light off. Water costs money. Do you think money grows on trees? I love you. I need a kiss. A bigger kiss. I will drive you there and I will pick you up.

Set your alarm clock. Did you set it? It's time to get up. Hurry, you'll be late. Can I help you? I love you. How was school? I need to talk to you. Can we talk? Don't forget your lunch money. What do you want for dinner tonight? I love you. Life isn't always fair. I don't care what your friend is doing. No. Yes. Maybe. We'll see. Ask your father. Go to sleep. Turn off the light. Okay, one more story. This is really the last one. (How precious they look when sleeping.)

I love you, my children. Sweet dreams.

My precious child, I am your heavenly father. I love you with all my being. Your love for your child is like my love for you. It is unconditional, powerful, beautiful, joyful, and also so much more. Understand that your children are like precious jewels. Your love for them cannot be matched by any other love. The love for your mother, father, sisters, brothers, husband or wife, friends, everyone who plays a part in your life is enormous.

Yet it pales in comparison with your love of child. This is a wondrous gift that humans possess. The gift of love for child. You could be the most kindhearted soul, a soul who would never harm even a buzzing insect; yet if anyone did harm to your own flesh, you have the capacity to kill. This is hard to believe of someone who is a gentle soul.

Love for child is all-powerful, all-consuming. I designed it to be this way, originally, to perpetuate the human species. A child who is loved is taken care of, is cherished, and is nurtured. This powerful love between mother and child is everlasting. Your children are like little flowers, growing and changing at such a rapid pace. Nurture them. Give them love, understanding, kindness, humor, a sense of spirituality. Read my words to them. Or simply tell them about God.

Make them familiar with my presence. They may remember mere glimpses of where they came from. These glimpses will be completely forgotten in no time at all. Your child, with your guidance, can accomplish great things, toward the greater good. They will grow spiritually in a magnificent way. Guide them in their growth experience. You will find it is tremendously rewarding.

> *God, I live on Long Island. A plane crashed just off our coast, killing everyone on board. I cannot imagine being in the air, knowing that the plane is going down and that death is imminent.*

The TWA Flight 800 disaster— how did these poor souls experience their death?

The passengers on Flight 800 did not experience any pain whatsoever. They knew that the plane was going down, but before they felt the impact of the crash, even long before the explosion that brought the plane down, these dear souls left the limits of their body. This happens often with a catastrophic event that claims the lives of many people at once.

Remember, I have mentioned the powers of many people combined. The great energy combined flowing from all the people on that plane enabled them to transcend their physical existence into the existence of the spiritual realm, before they even actually physically "died." I realize this is a new concept for you. I will try to explain this further.

The ability to leave your body before death is something that all people have. Many spiritual masters can control this and do control it on a regular basis. Some call it "astral projection." It is the ability to leave your physical body confined by time and space and enter a realm of heavenly existence. This requires tremendous desire and faith in the ability to do this.

When a person experiences this astral projection I speak of, they are actually still encumbered by their physical body, because their body is still physically alive. The experience is just a fleeting moment; they must always return to their living body and mind. Those who have mastered this technique have the ability to go anywhere they wish in the universe. The memory of their journey is always somewhat clouded. In fact, often during their experience they will keep telling themselves, "I will remember. . . . I will remember." This experience is through the altered state of the subconscious mind. It is always difficult to access the memories of the subconscious. Difficult but certainly not impossible. It is a very similar process to the one you have personally used to achieve communication with the divine force you call "God." If you desire to have this experience, you could.

Now, with regard to the people who perished in the Flight 800 crash—every one of them was aware of the impending disaster, for a split second. In this unbelievably brief moment, they made a decision among the entire group that they did not want to physically suffer. All together, all at once, they left their bodies behind. They could not return to their bodies, because in the next second these bodies ceased to physically live. Their next moments were filled with joy and beauty. Some individuals also experienced confusion over what just had happened to them. Some people pass to the other side more easily than others do. Some linger over their physical existence, watching in amazement their earthly demise. This is necessary for some.

Others are immediately welcomed by the most glorious light. The pure love of God is in this light. They are welcomed by all the people they loved in their many lives. A wonderful reunion is about to take place. There is no pain, no suffering, no evil—only all things that are good. They rejoice to be in such a wondrous place. They still can view what is going on in the Earthly plane of existence. They will always have this ability. Their existence on Earth was and is such an integral part of them that they will never completely break away from the experience. They will always watch over those they loved and left behind. With the passing of every person you loved, you are being watched over, guided, and protected by another angel in Heaven. You know that this is truth. These departed loved ones of yours are just as much a part of your life now in death as they were when they were alive. Acknowledge their presence in your life right now. It pleases them very much to be acknowledged in such a way.

I want to speak more about the process of death. You have tremendous power over how you experience your death. It can be an unbelievably beautiful experience and free from pain, if this is your desire. If you wish to leave your body before its physical demise, you can do this. Not all people choose to experience it this way. You have complete free will over the situation.

Death should not be feared. Death is just the beginning of a new life. It is a transition from one form to another. It is essential to your growth and progress. If it were not essential, you would be able to live forever. But it *is* essential. You may live many more lives, if that is your desire. Also know that if it is not your desire to come back to this great Earth to experience physical life, as you know it, then you do not have to come back. It is of *your* choosing, not God's.

Many who believe in reincarnation believe that God sends you back to the Earth because you need to learn lessons in order to progress toward the spiritual realm of Heaven. Know that these perfections are already there. They have been there from the very beginning. Your soul *is* perfection. If you wish to remain forevermore in the perfect love of this existence, you can. Many, many of you choose to experience physical life again and again. This physical life is part of my great gift to you. It is an imperfect life but there are moments of perfection that keep making you want to come back. The physical world of existence does possess wondrous joy. It is the ultimate affirmation of your existence when you are able to experience this joy that is forever prevalent in Heaven on Earth.

Those who believe that once you die you do not return to this physical existence are correct in *their* thinking. They, in all likelihood, will make the choice to remain in Heaven. This is their choice. Whatever is your truth, is simply *your truth*. Do not worry that your truth is not the same as their truth. All truths are beautiful and correct. All truths are one with God, but traditions are many. Mankind will someday realize this.

Religion should not divide; these differences are merely traditions. Spirituality will become the new way of thinking. Religions will remain intact but they will be viewed as traditions. This new spiritual thinking will enable the world to rapidly progress toward universal peace and harmony. There will no longer be prejudice or discrimination towards another. The power struggle will not exist any longer. It will be understood that all traditions lead to God. No one tradition is more worthy of God's love than another. God's love is for *all*.

With this newfound understanding among all of mankind, a new civilization will be born. "On Earth as it is in Heaven" will be realized. How can all this change come about? The undeniable, all-powerful, pure essence of *love*. This change will not take place overnight. How long it takes depends on many factors. When will this pure love exist in the hearts of all mankind? I cannot answer this question. It is completely within the power of the masses. Choosing to make the transformation occur is their own free will. It will begin with small numbers of people. Once it has begun it is only a matter of time before the ultimate goal is realized.

This is what your destiny is, what everyone's destiny is. It will begin with an awareness; with this newfound awareness will come change; with this change will come unity. With this newfound unity will come understanding and compassion. In turn this new spiritual awareness will be realized. Love will exist in the hearts of all. Pure love at all times. When this love is ever-present it will be possible for the physical world and the spiritual world to become one. These two worlds will merge into one dimension. This is the ultimate realization of mankind's mission. We will talk more of this merging.

Wow! Dear God, I asked a simple question regarding the experience of death. That was some answer! A beautiful and inspiring answer. Thank you. It is remarkable. Just when I think that you cannot "wow" me with your answers, you prove me wrong. I will always be in awe of your gentle reassurance and your wisdom. Thank you so much for providing these answers to me.

My child, it pleases me very much that I can still "wow" you. Take notice of the beautiful sunset I have in store for you this evening! Sky of fire and tranquillity. The warmth, the love spreads across the horizon, reflecting on the mirror of water below. Watch the gull flying overhead, looking at the sky with wonder. Appreciate the wonder of the sunset, appreciate the wonder of the water, and appreciate the wonder of the gull flying overhead. Appreciate the beauty all around you. Take a moment to drink it all into your very soul. It feels so good. Does it not? Take the time to do this on a regular basis. Feed your soul, as you feed your body. Admire the beauty of nature. This beauty is all around you. Take the time to notice it. Rejoice in it.

This sun is your personal symbol of God's love. Did you realize this before? This sun shines down on you, ever-present. Even at night the sun is ever-present, you simply cannot see it. That does not mean it is not there. The sun is always, eternally present. Bask in its rays, feel the warmth, the fire within. This sun gives you life. It gives life to all living things; without it you would cease to exist. It is no wonder that early civilizations worshiped the sun as God. They were correct in their thinking the sun is God. All things are God. My love is everywhere you

look, all things. Take the time to notice this, every day.
Recognize the wonder of God's ever-present love all around
you. It pleases me very much that I can "wow" you!

*Most of the questions that I ask God are relative
to all of humanity. Throughout this book I have asked
questions that are on a more personal level as well.
After all, this is my truth, my experience. Everyone
has profound experiences of a spiritual nature.
Whether or not everyone acknowledges these experiences is another thing.*

*Throughout my life, I knew I wanted to someday
be a mother. When I did realize that dream at the age
of twenty-five, I experienced a profound spiritual
experience. I realize that I am not the first woman to
experience birth; yet when our son Jake was born, I
felt that it was such a miracle of God—so unique, so
marvelous. I was in complete awe from the experience.
I'm sure many women (and men) are affected in such a
way.*

*The first night after my son was born, I lay in
my hospital bed exhausted and at the same time elat-
ed. I had never felt so at peace, so good, so happy. I
fell into a deep sleep. I began to have terrible nightmares. I dreamt that my son had a defect in his
heart—that he was in danger and had to be taken
away to another hospital to have some kind of emer-
gency surgery. My dream was vivid and so very
frightening. I thought I would lose my mind with the
terror I was experiencing. Just as they were taking
my precious new baby away in an ambulance, I
awoke. I let out a loud gasp, as if I were drowning
somehow.*

*A nurse must have been just entering my room,
because she came running over to me. I began crying.
Big sobs came from me. I was so relieved it was just a
dream. The nurse remained with me. She asked me
what was wrong. Before I told her my story, in a split*

second I thought to myself that it was probably some irrational fear that I was experiencing as a new mother. I thought, "Please God, don't let me have that dream again." It was just too powerful, too scary.

I then told the nurse what my nightmare was about. She looked at me really strangely. Her mouth was hanging open. She ran from my room. I was very confused at the time. I had no idea why she was acting so strangely. When she came back she had another nurse with her. They calmly told me that what I had described to them had just happened to a woman on the other side of the maternity floor. Now I understood why my experience was so real. I truly felt this poor woman's pain and horror.

The two nurses and I agreed to pray for this newborn baby—to pray that his heart would be repaired and that he would have a chance at life. After that night I did not see the nurses again. I desperately wanted to know what happened to that baby. I didn't even know what the woman's name was. All I had was my dream.

On my last day at the hospital, as I was getting ready to bring my new son home, in walked one of the nurses. This time I got her name, Barbara. Barbara told me that the baby was going to make it. They didn't know yet what the long-term prognosis would be, but so far it looked very promising. That was all she could tell me. I asked her if she could reveal who the mother was, so that I could meet her. I wanted to continue my prayer for her and her baby. Barbara told me she could not give me that information. It would be a breach of ethics. I was disappointed, but I understood. My son Jake is a strong, healthy, bright, and beautiful eight-year-old. I have often thought of that other baby boy who was born on the same day as my son. I wonder if he is all right. Did he grow up strong? I wonder what the significance of my dream was, why I had a connection with this mother and child.

Is there any significance to this dream I had?

Yes, there is significance. The experience you had affected you. To this day, you remember it and can recollect the finest details. You can still feel the horror of your baby being taken away. Remember, I spoke of the importance of your dreams. Through your dreams and nightmares you may experience that which is not good. Certainly, this dream was so vivid you experienced it as real. Your reality was just as true as the woman's reality who experienced it physically and with the conscious mind/experience.

Of course, once you awoke, the reality dissolved as you came to find that it was only your subconscious mind experiencing it in a dream state. How relieved you were. Yet to your surprise, you found out that some dear woman had to live this terrible dream. Your heart went out to her. You made a connection with her. You conversed with others regarding her problem. This woman had many people praying for the welfare of her child. The loving energy going to this precious child enabled its surgery to be successful. This baby boy did grow strong! This baby boy is living in a nearby town.

God is not a fortune-teller, I cannot tell you where to specifically find this boy. But remember that if you truly desire to find him, your paths will cross. Always be open to the synchronicities of your life. These everyday, mysterious "coincidences" will always lead you to the information that you are seeking. You will encounter this boy and his mother at a place where other boys of the same age will be. The two boys, your son Jake and the other, will have a friend in common. Be alert for this experience.

Meet and greet those you encounter with love in your heart. Send your loving energy outward. If you do this, you can trust that the information you are seeking will come to you. This works in all situations. You know this works for you. So many times you have been gently led to that which you seek. This is of your own doing. Is it not marvelous, the power of your being?

You, as well as all mankind, have not even begun to tap

into the power you all inherently possess. Not even one-tenth of this power is being utilized by the average human being. The advancement of your species will astound you when your true potential is reached. In time it will be.

In the meantime, pay attention to all your dreams, all your nightmares as well. They do have significance. You may not even realize what the dream is trying to tell you, what reality it is trying to create for you. But know that everyone needs to experience truth through his or her nightly slumber. Now, on that note—sleep, my dear one. Sweet dreams.

On this day my husband Giacomo and I will be married for eleven years. It is hard for me to believe. The time went by so fast. We were high school sweethearts. We grew up together. We share something very special, my husband and I. He is my first and only true love. I don't think too many people can say this today. My husband and I still live in the same little town we grew up in. I would not be surprised if we contentedly lived our whole lives here. Over the years we have seen many couples whom we thought would be together forever, sadly divorce.

Why is it that some people can and do stay in a marriage for their entire lives while others "bail out" and divorce? I realize that some marriages could never work out. But I believe that all couples encounter problems along the way. All have their ups and downs typical of life in general. Certainly, my husband and I have had moments of bliss and moments where we probably hated each other despite our constant love for one another. I know that we will always remain committed to this marriage of ours. It is of utmost importance to me and to my husband. So many couples divorce these days. I do not know the exact statistics, but I know the divorce rate is very high.

What can so many failed marriages be attributed to?

Marriage is the sacred union of man and woman. Marriage in many ways has lost its sacredness. Many couples set up homes together before they make a commitment of marriage to each other. They live as man and wife in all respects. The only exception is that a true commitment has not taken place. This absolute commitment is the underlying factor that holds a marriage together. Like the bloom of a beautiful flower, passion can fade. Love, respect, trust, honesty are all important factors in a "good marriage." But even when all these attributes are present, if the couple does not truly have a commitment, a lifelong commitment to one another, then the marriage can cease to exist.

This commitment is something taken very seriously by those who are partners for life. No matter what tragedy they endure, no matter what success or failure they experience, they know that they will experience it together. They even know that if their love or trust is jeopardized, they will endure. They are in this for the long haul and will not back down from their commitment to one another. The trials and tribulations a couple goes through on the path of life together strengthen their bonds to one another. When two people are truly committed to each other for life, they have a spiritual union as well as social. A spiritual union is a union of souls. Every soul has a soul mate—a soul that complements a like soul so perfectly that they are meant to be together. You will encounter your soul mate many, many times in your many lives.

A successful marriage does not necessarily mean you are with your soul mate. If a commitment has been made and true love is in the hearts of both parties, the marriage can be successful. A soul on the path to all things good can live happily with many other souls. This is their nature. Your soul mate has nothing to do with gender. Nor does your soul mate have anything to do with sexual attraction. You have been man and woman. You possess many qualities that are inherently feminine and masculine. These two qualities are integral parts of your existence. When I speak of a soul mate, this is a soul who was created as you were created. All souls are smaller pieces of the larger universal energy force you call God. Some pieces are very similar and alike in their complex makeup. They are like a matched pair. They work perfectly together.

When you encounter your soul mate in the physical dimension on Earth, you can accomplish great things together. You can especially make great strides in your soul's evolutionary process. You are like one in your perception of the universe. You possess the same ideals. You may be very different personalities, from very different backgrounds and upbringing, yet there is a sense of perfect balance. Together you are perfection. In your physical life, if you have the great pleasure of knowing each other (which is very possible) you will shine brightly when you are in the presence of your soul mate. Your energy level will always be very high. You will constantly uplift each other to a higher level. You will bring out the very best in each other, in all the time you spend together. Your soul mate can be anyone. Your best friend, your husband or wife, your sister. You are very blessed if you have a relationship with your soul mate. When you are both on the earth plane together at the same time, you will know this in your subconscious mind. Your intuitive sense will guide you to seek out this person.

You are not always together on the earth plane at the same time. Sometimes you simply miss each other, like passing ships in the night. If you have a relationship with this soul mate, you will know it. You will experience unbelievable joy and love whenever you are with this person. If you feel you are in a marriage that is a commitment for life, you are blessed. If this marriage is primarily of love, you are doubly blessed. Hence, if it is a marriage of true love, then all other godly attributes will follow: honesty, trust, compassion, respect. This indeed is a happy marriage, a happy lifetime together with someone you have chosen to be with "till death do you part."

If you have been lucky enough to find your soul mate in this lifetime, and your relationship advances to the sacred ritual of marriage, then you will surely be immensely and forevermore blessed by this union. Know and understand that if you do not feel you married your soul mate, this does not mean that your marriage is doomed. Every soul has the immense capacity to love. Every soul is working towards the manifestation of the potential pure love, which exists universally among all souls.

If you are on a path that leads toward the greater good of mankind, if you are contributing towards this greater good, chances are you will be blessed with a happy, lifelong marriage. If you desire to experience marriage in this way, if it is of the utmost importance to you, then you will create this for yourself.

How important is it to set goals?

You and you alone are responsible for your own happiness. When you set goals for yourself, you lay out a road map for your own success. People will get only what they seek.

They will accomplish only that which they choose to accomplish for themselves. You are the motivating factor. Know yourself well. Know what is important to you. Know your likes and dislikes. Do not waver from your own truths. Do not be swayed by others' belief systems. Your truth is your own. Be aware of what you can and cannot do and of what you can do well—especially of what you love doing. Choose a lifestyle or career that reflects what you love doing. Work hard but play hard as well.

Balance is essential when working towards your goals. It is very important that you always have a goal that you are striving towards. These goals that you set for yourself give life meaning and long-term direction. The goals you set can be small and short-term, or they can take a lifetime to achieve. Strive to achieve all that you want out of life. Work towards developing your spiritual nature. Through this you will be able to determine what your life's purpose is. Find the joy in everything you do. Even the dreary aspects of life possess hidden joy. Search out this joy. If you really try, you can always find it. Strive to make every aspect of your life a triumph, an accomplishment. There is great power in achieving the goals you set for yourself. Your confidence level will rise. You will know no limits. Take the power in creating a life that is both joyful and filled with love.

Every day is a new opportunity, a fresh start to be the best day possible. You will never have the moment of *now* again. Take advantage of each moment. Realize the potential of every moment. Live every moment. Have an appreciation of the present moment. Know that you will not have this moment again. Spend more time with the people and things that bring you the most happiness and contentment. Spend less time on the pastimes and the people that don't bring you love or joy.

This sounds very simple, but learn to say no more often. This is a difficult thing for many people to do, yourself included. But it is detrimental to the soul to be doing things in your life out of guilt or obligation. God is not telling you that you should be selfish in your actions, but if you are trapped into doing things that you really are not happy with, your soul will not be free. If your soul is not free, it cannot grow. It cannot experience love in its purest form. What a tragedy this is.

Strive always to live with joy in your heart, your soul, your being. Plan to live your life in this manner. Set goals for yourself that bring you towards this joyful existence. This is *your* life, live the life you were born to live.

I just had an experience that I believe was a response to a request I made. You absolutely must be careful what you ask for. You will undoubtedly receive whatever it is. In the last few days even though I have been communicating with God, still asking questions and still receiving wonderful and beautiful answers, I could not help thinking, "I wish God would give me a sign, as I have received signs in the past of God's existence."

Well, I do believe I just experienced this sign. I am a fortunate woman to be able to sit here at my desk in my basement typing this on my computer. Just minutes ago I awoke at eight-thirty A.M., I lay in bed for quite a while, slowly waking up. I got up, let my pets (two dogs and cat) out. Greeted my son, who was also awake. As I stood there waiting for the dogs to do their morning ritual, I was thinking about how bad the mosquitoes are this year. I thought, "God, what did you have in mind when you created the mosquito?" I let the dogs in and went back to bed to linger for just a little longer.

All of a sudden I remembered that the night before I had been writing. I had, as many times before, lit a small scented candle while I was working. I went to bed around two A.M., and I forgot to blow out the flame! My thought was, "Oh my God!" I flew down the stairs. As soon as I got to the first level of my house I smelled the unbelievable aroma of the wax burning. How had I not smelled this before?

I ran down the second flight of stairs into the basement. There I found the candle. The flame was about six inches above the small glass cup that holds the wax. I quickly blew out the candle and in a loud voice said, "Thank you, God!" I touched the cup. It was very hot. The area around the cup was very hot. Inches away were papers, and a general mess. I realized how lucky I was that I did not have a fire. What an unbelievably close call it was—too close. I couldn't help thinking that this was an affirmation of God's presence in my life. How wonderful it is to know this.

As I was rejoicing in this knowledge, a big bug flew into the room. The bug was flying erratically, bumping into things. I thought it was a beetle, but I was not sure. Since my communication with God began, I have gone to great lengths to set bugs free rather than squashing them. I thought to myself that I had to catch this bug and let it go outside. I got a cup. I thought I would scoop it up when it landed on the ceiling above me. It kept flying near the ceiling but it would not land. Its motion would not stop. I thought, "How am I going to catch this bug?"

With that in my head I told the bug, "I am trying to help you, I want to set you free—fly into the cup. Now!" With that, the bug flew into the cup. I put my hand over the top and said, "Thank you, bug." I went upstairs, opened my back door, walked outside, and turned the cup over. The bug landed on my deck and I thought, "How stupid, after all this, I killed it." It lay there motionless. I could see that it was a large and beautiful brown beetle. I gently touched it with my index finger and then it flew away. I was happy, I saved yet another bug.

I couldn't help thinking that the flame and the bug have some significance, that perhaps they were the sign that I had been hoping for from God. It just

*seemed too weird to me to not matter. I believe that we
notice things for a reason. When we take notice it is
because something significant has occurred.*

Is there meaning to this strange event?

Yes, of course. Did you not ask for a sign? Your angels
remained ever vigilant through the night, keeping that flame
from spreading. These angels sent from me, your God, will
tirelessly protect you through the night. They are with you
always when you need them. Your life is precious, dear one.
You have a mission in this life. You are not going anywhere
until this mission is carried out and completed. Be careful,
dear one, you do have free will to make your own mistakes.
Do not light a candle and walk away from it. This message
that I was trying to convey is trust in God. Trust that God
protects his children from harming themselves.

You are sometimes your own worst enemy. You have
made a connection with the divine source of my enormous
love for you. This is a very good thing. You have tapped into the
unending source of this love. I watch over all my children
even if they have not made a connection with me. But I cannot guide my children gently through life if they will not let
me. You have opened up to this guidance. You have complete trust in God that all things will work out. You have
complete faith in my love for you. You know this love exists
eternally and is ever-present forevermore.

This sign I sent to you is a confirmation of your faith.
The beetle, which I sent to you, is a confirmation of *my* faith
in you. I have faith that you will do the right thing. I have
faith that you are working towards the greater good of all
mankind. In setting that little bug free, you demonstrated your
love for the world, your love for all of God's people and all of
God's creatures, even the small flying bug. You saw the beauty in that bug—the love that even a mere bug can possess.
Remember, I told you to recognize the love in everything.

There is love present in it *all*. This love is often hidden and must be discovered, but it is always there.

I have tremendous faith in *you*, my precious child, that you can make a difference in this world, that you can encourage others to make a difference as well. It is through your example, your loving heart, your loving gesture, your kind words and actions that you can most effectively encourage others to make this difference. When you uplift the people whom you encounter, they will in turn uplift many others. This will set into motion a great transformation in which everyone is striving to uplift the world to a higher level, towards this pure love I keep speaking of. I realize that in many of our conversations, I always return to this basic thought, this basic concept.

Your soul's progress, the progress of all souls is working towards the greater good of all mankind. In this greater good, pure love exists. This is the goal of all souls.

I will go back to this idea again and again. This is truly all that there is. This is what everything boils down to. This one undeniable truth is universal in every single human being. Regardless of your race, your religion, your tradition, your social class—regardless of anything else, this is *your* truth. This is *everyone's* truth.

Oh—to answer your question, "What did you have in mind when you created the mosquito?" How would you not know the glory of the butterfly?

Thank you, dear God!

You're very welcome, my dear child.

It is interesting that through my communication with God I have had some of my beliefs altered by the experience. Growing up, I always believed in the power and the wrath of God. I thought that God was loving, but that God also punished us for our sins. My picture of God was a vengeful one. Part of my conscience was developed out of a fear of God. I am coming to realize that none of this is true. God is all-loving. God does not pass judgment, only we pass judgment.

In having a conscience we strive toward the greater good of mankind. This movement toward the greater good is derived from God, but God gives us complete free will to make our own decisions, our own mistakes. God does not punish us for our mistakes. God hopes that we learn from them.

Through this great learning we experience tremendous growth. Through this growth the world slowly begins to awaken and transform. We are in the midst of this awakening. I am personally having a spiritual awakening of my own. I sense that many are having or will be having this experience in the very near future. This is very exciting to me. I always dreaded the coming of the new millennium. I thought it would be the end of the world. I no longer feel this way.

I have a new sense of hope for the world's future—the future of my children and my children's children. I will be eternally grateful for this new sense of hope. I no longer fear the new millennium. I look forward to it! I hope that this book helps others to see the hope—to have faith in this hope of the future. I have found out so many wondrous things through my communication with God.

In the beginning my sister, Andrea, said to me, "These are your beliefs." I thought, "Yes, that is true but many of the questions I am asking, I am asking because I do not know the answers. I have no idea what the answers are, that is why I am doing the asking." With every answer, I received a message of a gentle, reassuring love. I know that I am conversing with a source that is of the highest power. I am convinced that this is the true source. Others might dispute this. I can bet my life on it. I have bet my life on it. I know this is my truth, more than I have ever known anything in my entire life.

God told me that all truths are beautiful, all truths lead to God's love. Religious beliefs and traditions are many, but truth is one. I get a little confused about this. If all truths are right, why am I being told of these specific truths that God is speaking to me? They are my truths. Are they someone else's as well? I know people who are religious fanatics. They are specifically of the Christian faith. They believe that only those who recognize Christ as the savior will enter into the kingdom of Heaven. This is certainly their truth. This is not my truth.

I have been told that all may enter the kingdom of Heaven. I like to believe that this is true. I cannot imagine God denying access to any of his children. God told me that he loves not one individual more than another. This is a fair and just God. This is my God. If God is giving me these messages to give to the world, is this truth above others? I do not want to create any problems out of this communication. I only want to help the world through it. How can all truths be right, and my truth be right as well?

All truths do not agree.
How can they all be right?

Reality within the confines of the physical world is an illusion. Everyone creates their own reality. How you perceive your reality is *your truth*. Your ego does not really exist. It is not the true self. Neither is the physical body or mind. Your existence is not based on your accomplishments or the reality that you have created. You are really a divine soul. This soul lives eternally. It has no beginning and no end. It does change form, but it is ever-present. It cannot ever be destroyed. Your human experience, the physical existence on Earth, is but a temporary thing. You will always return to God, to the *universal truth*. This truth is the underlying truth of truths. This truth is *love*.

All the great religions and philosophies of the world contain the path to this truth—different yet equally valid paths.

You can't experience the truth of another person without feeling love towards that person. Through this love comes understanding. Understanding and love go together, hand in hand. The truths I am telling you (the answers to your questions) contain everyone's truths, every belief system that there is. I am telling you that all these truths are real. They have been created by each individual believer. But as I said before, this reality is an illusion. It is transitory; it is always going through some change. It changes to fit the needs of society at large for a different time and place.

The message is slightly different, but the underlying truth remains. This underlying truth is the truth of truths. It is timeless. It cannot change. This truth will exist forever into eternity. This *big* truth is love. The message you are bringing suits the times and needs of the present society.

For the advancement of the soul it is necessary that all truths be recognized as true; it is also necessary to accept each person's truth as truth. I hope this is not too confusing. I hope I have answered your question in words you can understand. Sometimes it is difficult to explain that which cannot be explained. Trust that your truth is valid. Your truth is important—not more important than any other truth, but still of utmost importance to your soul's progression, along with the progression of many other like souls.

These like souls will search for this book. This book will find them when they need it most in their lives. When they are most ready to hear these words, when they can benefit from them the most, the words will come to them. Your writings will not be for all people. Some will disagree with what you are trying to say. But many others will embrace what you are saying. These individuals will be transfixed to the information contained herein. It is these people who will benefit from your experience. These individuals will advance in their spiritual development. This is what they are seeking in their lives. You are not responsible for their advancement. I am not responsible for their advancement.

Your soul grows when you discover the great gifts that God has given each and every one of you. Make full use of these gifts by serving others. Your soul thrives when you give to others. This book is your labor of love. It is the gift you are giving to the people with whom you share your life. It is the gift you would like to give to many others, to those who would like and need to receive it.

Rejoice in knowing that you are reaching your own human potential. You are using your God-given gifts freely with their greatest and grandest purpose in mind. Do not stray from this path. Remain steadfast in your actions. Love is the greatest manifestation of the soul's growth. There are several other attributes that are essential to this growth: forgiveness, compassion, charity, patience, courage, wisdom, and kindness.

When your soul has truly evolved, you are able to live a life that balances all these attributes. Continue to work towards this balance. You have far to go. Ultimately you will arrive at the destination that you are seeking. It is simply a matter of time.

God, my belief in you is steadfast and strong. With every year that passes, my belief expands to an even higher and more beautiful level. I find it so difficult to believe that anyone could deny the existence of God. I have never actually met and spoken with an atheist. I would be intrigued by their viewpoint, I am sure.

I do not understand how any living person could not recognize the presence of a universal creative force, a higher intelligence working through myself and all people towards the greater good of humanity. Are there truly people who do not believe?

Are there really atheists?

Dear child, I have many monikers. You call me "God." I speak to you in words that you can grasp and understand.

Others call me by many other different names, and embrace and recognize me in endless manners. There is not a single soul I have created who does not recognize my existence. If they acknowledge their own existence, they acknowledge God. Simply living your life is an acknowledgment of God.

If you believe in yellow daffodils, you believe in God. If you believe in a fiery, living sunrise, you believe in God. If you believe in a precious infant suckling at the breast of its loving mother, you believe in God. If you believe in a sparkling, multifaceted diamond, you believe in God. If you believe in the great Earth and all its inhabitants, you believe in God. If you believe in the moon, the stars, the planets, and the heavens above, you believe in God.

If you can feel the warm caress of the sun's rays, you believe in God. If you can taste the sweetness of honey, you believe in God. If you can smell the salty spray from the great oceans, you believe in God. If you can see the rainbow in the sky, beautiful colors blending together in a fantastic bow of light, you believe in God. If you can hear the sound of rain falling and the crack of a thunderous storm, you absolutely, undeniably believe in God! All these glorious wonders are proof of God. Do you exist? Yes! Then God exists.

How can I achieve the goals I have set for myself?

Take a risk to be different. Turn your ideas, your inspirations, into action. This requires your energy, your commitment, and your courage. To act requires risk—risk of not fitting in the same mold as everyone else. This risk can be scary at times. When you began writing this book, you took a risk. You risked ridicule, judgment, and condemnation. The words came to you as thoughts, as inspiration. You took action and wrote them down. You could have dismissed the ideas—the words that were spoken to you by God. All risk requires courage as well as determination. You can have the best, the grandest of intentions, but if you do not turn these ideas of yours into action, they become wasted. Wasted inspiration is a tragedy. All intentions have the potential for being realized.

Your actions will always speak louder than words or any thoughts you may have. Without a word you can comfort a loved one in pain. Through your embrace, your gentle touch, your smile, and your loving gesture—these actions are far more powerful for providing comfort and healing. No matter what you *feel* in your heart, no matter what you *think* and undeniably know as fact, no matter what potential for talent lies waiting within you—only your *actions* can bring life to them.

Through your actions you gain tremendous wisdom. You are able to realize what is really important to you. In realizing what is important, you gain tremendous insight. You cannot get through a dense forest of trees, shrubs, flowers, and tangled vegetation merely by thinking about it. You may be inspired by an idea on the easiest, most efficient way to get through that forest and to the other side. Until you take the first step, the first action, you cannot begin to get to the blessed clearing that awaits you on the other side of this forest.

Taking action to accomplish any great task requires you to transform the whole process into a series of tiny, baby steps towards your goal. You must trust in your own infinite potential for reaching your goal. When you work towards smaller goals within the ultimate larger goal, it is possible to achieve your greatest desires.

Goals that are worthwhile and important to you always require tremendous effort and often sacrifice. You are trying to become more than you were before. This is a big undertaking! Hold your original vision, which is true to your heart/soul. Make sure that the goal is truly of utmost importance to you or you will not devote the energy needed to accomplish it. It must be worth the effort, worth the sacrifice. This requires thinking and reflection on your part, before you even set sight on a specific goal.

I have told you many times that you have the ability within yourself to create whatsoever you desire. Remember the word "d-e-s-i-r-e." Move towards goals that excite you, motivate you, attract you—those that touch your heart, that you desire with all your being. Be passionate about your goals, your desires. Don't depend on others to tell you what you should or should not be doing. Only *you* know what is best for *you*. Rely on yourself.

This does not mean that others cannot help you along the way. It simply means that you and *you* alone are responsible for your own actions and your own happiness. Always "to thine own self be true." This is a wise old adage. You and you alone will experience the great glory within when you reach your highest goals.

After this answer God spoke to me in a curious way regarding goals. I found it amusing.

God does not keep score with the goals you reach. Your life is not a soccer match. Pursue your dreams. Pursue your highest goals. Do this for yourself. Always strive to reinvent yourself, to make yourself a new and improved version! When on the field of life you will not always "score." If you had fun—you won! The greatest feeling of joy is not necessarily at the moment you reach your goal. You will realize in retrospect, upon reflection, that the greatest joy was taking those baby steps to reach your goal.

A Test

Many years ago my sister Andrea introduced me to an insightful, fun "test." It consists of just five simple questions. Over the years I have given this test to many people. Every single time, the test taker has been astounded by the perceptions these simple questions reveal. I want to share this with you. I encourage you to try it out for yourself, try it on others. You will be amazed at the insight it will give you. Just for the fun of it, answer the five questions below. Don't cheat!

Question 1: What is your favorite color? Describe it with at least four adjectives.

Question 2: What is your favorite animal? Describe it with at least four adjectives.

Question 3: Would you rather be in a puddle? An ocean? Or a bathtub? Describe it with at least four adjectives.

Question 4: If you were in a small, dark room with no windows or doors and couldn't get out, describe with at least four adjectives how you would feel.

Question 5: What is the one thing in your life that you look at with the most wonderful feeling? Describe it with at least four adjectives.

I took this test about three years ago when my daughter was just a baby. I am telling you my responses so that you can interpret what these answers mean. My answers are simply a model used to give an explanation.

The adjectives you use to describe your favorite color also describe how you perceive yourself. In question number two, the adjectives describe how you think others perceive, or "see," you. In question number three, you have three responses to choose from: puddle, ocean, or bathtub. Your choice is in reference to your sexual preferences—the adjectives describe how you feel about sex. In question number four, the adjectives describe how you feel regarding death. And in question number five, the adjectives describe how you feel about God.

My responses:

Question 1: What is your favorite color?
Blue.

Describe it with at least four adjectives.
Calm, striking, spiritual, conservative.

This is how I perceive myself, a very accurate perception.

Question 2: What is your favorite animal?
Cat.

Describe it with at least four adjectives.
Smart, independent, affectionate, beautiful.
This is how I think others see me. It's funny, because I probably would not admit (even to myself) that others see me as beautiful. But with reflection, I admit it's exactly true.

Question 3: Would you rather be in a puddle? An ocean? Or a bathtub?
Ocean.

Describe it with at least four adjectives.
Sacred, exciting, relaxing, enjoyable.

This is how I feel about sex. Amazing. Every description is exactly right.

Question 4: If you were in a small, dark room with no windows or doors and couldn't get out, describe with at least four adjectives how you would feel.
Panic, fear, alone, hopeful.

This is the way I feel about death, very accurate, very true.

Question 5: What is the one thing in your life that you look at with the most wonderful feeling?
My children.

Describe it with at least four words.
Precious, beautiful, love, joy.

These words truly do describe how I feel about God. Isn't it nice to know that we all view God in the same light that we view what gives us the most wonderful feeling?

I hope you enjoyed this "test." Have fun with it. Try it with your friends and family. They will think it is pretty amazing.

Can science and religion coexist peacefully?

Science and religion have always provoked emotional, intense, and sometimes inspirational debates and/or disputes. The dogma of many religions cannot be true if the research of scientists is true as well. Man's progression towards the greater good requires science. Science is an integral part of the ultimate goal—an existence based on pure love. The true knowledge of God is the great unknown. Science brings the unknown to the reality of humanity.

Science and knowledge have made great progress in this century. Consider the great mysteries that have been discovered and realized. How many great inventions have been brought to light? How many new inventions are increasing in number day by day? Material science and the increasing wealth of knowledge and learning will truly amaze the great masses of people. Great progress and great wonders will be revealed.

In the past, religion has been the opponent of science. This has been a conflict without resolution. Many believe that science is the destroyer of the foundations of religion. Now understand that the new spiritual awakening I speak of is essential to the progression towards unity of a new world order—a union of all beliefs, an appreciation and respect for all truths.

With this newfound spirituality it will be discovered that religions are mere traditions, mere mythology, trying to explain the great mystery that is God—trying to explain the unexplainable. Future scientists of the universe will attempt to prove God's existence. The great bounties of knowledge from the spiritual realm cannot ever be fully realized until the entire world is operating in a state of pure, beautiful, godly love.

I find astrology to be very interesting, even though I know very little about it. I realize that even some United States presidents have relied on astrologers to guide them in decision making.

Do the stars in the heavens influence our earthly existence?

Oh yes. The stars do indeed have a relationship with the Earth and all its inhabitants. Think of the great universe as a living, breathing entity, a body, if you will. Every component that makes up this universe is a part of the sum of it. Your body, like the universe, is made up of many smaller, working components. You are not aware of the particular inner workings of your liver, your heart, your spleen, and your kidneys, yet these organs are all essential to the whole sum of the body's existence. The stars, the planets, the smaller moons and asteroids are all integral components of the greater heavenly body. All components in your physical body, as well as the heavenly bodies, have been designed by God to be linked and connected with one another. Through this connection there is a greater strength of the whole body. All components are intermingled. They have great influence over one another.

This intermingling is for the mutual aid and benefit of the whole. This intermingling of the great stars and all the other various heavenly parts has cause and effect. The source of this cause and effect is a spiritual source. A source that is derived from the divine being of God. This spiritual influence affects the physical world. The spiritual dimension and physical dimension are forever linked to one another. My children cannot deny the spiritual influence on the physical world.

Everything that exists within the universe is a form of energy. These different forms vibrate at different rates, constantly expanding and contracting. There is a cycle that works as law with regard to all forms of energy. The sun rises and then it sets. The moon waxes and wanes, affecting the tides on the Earth. The tides themselves have an ebb and flow. The seasons change—winter, spring, summer, and fall. Forever the seasons come and go, filled with everlasting change. All things have a rise and a fall. All things have a cycle. Sometimes these cycles take a great amount of time.

Be patient, dear children. Just as the sky grows darkest before the dawn, your life has its darkest points before the light rises from beneath the horizon. In this light you will be riding the wave, moving in a positive direction in your life. These waves rise and fall. There is a natural rhythm working in your life. Appreciate and recognize the inner workings of this rhythm.

Take advantage of whatever point in the cycle you find yourself. Find harmony within your cycles. There is always and forever change and growth in your physical existence. These cycles move you along the path to the greater good. To know and understand joy, one must also understand sorrow. These are merely cycles. These cycles are present in everyone's life. Whatever rises must fall, and whatever falls shall rise *again*. All things will happen in good time. Have patience and trust that this is so.

Realize that your life is like one great circle. There is the spring of youth, filled with promise and rebirth. There is the carefree summer of adolescent years. There are the years of fall to harvest the fruits of your labors. And then there is the winter of your final years, as your life nears the end of the great cycle.

It is during these winter years that you have quiet time for reflection. This is a time for slowing down and reviewing the past seasons. The stars in the heavens are forever present in the seasons of your life. The stars change position in relationship to the great Earth. They change as the seasons change. One influences the other.

All human beings have physical life on the earth plane, which eventually moves into the season of winter. Here this physical life withers, fades, and dies. But spring is eternal. Spring is found in the kingdom of Heaven. Here lies the promise. Here lies renewal. Here lies a new beginning. In this springtime, new seeds may be planted, with a sense of renewed hope for the new cycle before you. You may improve on this new cycle with the wisdom gained from the previous. The cycles are ever-present on Earth as it is in Heaven. The seasons/cycles form a great circle in their changing, and always come back around.

I have been so blessed to experience "angelic" encounters with the passing of every loved one I have ever lost. I am fortunate to have had these experiences. Whenever a person you loved deeply dies, you suffer. You may realize that the person who died is no longer suffering but is in a beautiful, wonderful, loving place with God. This does not help you to miss them any less.

When I was fourteen my great-grandmother Marie passed away. She was eighty-five years old. I was not ready to let her go. I loved her so much. This was my first experience with death. My faith in God was not as strong as it is now. When she died, I worried that maybe this life was all there is. I worried that with the dying of her body, she ceased to exist. I was very sad and I knew I would miss her terribly. I really was not sure if I would ever see her again.

The day after her funeral I sat on my bed contemplating all my feelings towards death and towards my beloved Grandma Marie. Deep in thought, I felt a presence come into the room. I knew instantly that it was Grandma. She sat next to me on the bed. I never actually saw her, but I could smell her scent and I could feel the warmth of her "body" sitting next to me. She touched my hand. I could feel this touch as if it were really true. We then had a mental conversation. The words were unheard with the ears, but they were heard with the heart. She called me by my pet name and said, "Nonno, I am fine, I am happy, I am at peace. It is a beautiful place I am going to. I need to go now. I love you very much."

With that, she was gone. In our conversation I told her to go and that I loved her very much as well. It was such a beautiful, wonderful experience! All my sadness left me. I knew she was okay. I knew she was not dead and that her soul lived on. I was forever changed by this experience. Slowly, my fear of death began to fade away. I knew in my heart that there was much more to our existence than this life on Earth. The whole reason for grieving, the ritual of the funeral and the mourning that follows, is for the people who are left behind, not for the dear soul who departed.

After this event, I have been blessed to have an experience each time someone I loved passed on to the other side. I thank God for every one of these encounters. When my mother-in-law Marianna died, it was unbelievably painful. I felt so bad for my dear husband. I was miserable. I could not even imagine how he felt.

The evening of the day she died, I had a terrible nightmare. I dreamt that we were all at the hospital trying to visit my mother-in-law, and no one could find her. We were all there, all her loved ones, and not one of us could find where she was hidden. We were all so upset in the dream. We searched and searched. Our efforts were futile and we never did find her. This dream disturbed me. I wasn't upset enough that she had died—now I was having nightmares that she was *lost! For three nights in a row I had this same dream. Each time, we wandered the halls searching and searching for her. It was so distressing, so frustrating. I told my husband about these dreams. I could not imagine their meaning. I was looking for healing and instead kept having dreams of the most frustrating and dismal nature.*

Finally, on the fourth night I awoke suddenly from a dream. It was very early in the morning, maybe four or five o'clock. I remembered my dream clearly. We were all still frantically searching for Marianna—running through the halls, calling her name. Finally, in another part of the hospital, a place we had never been to before, we walked into a beautiful room. It was shining brightly. Everything was white, but it was luminous and glowing as well.

Sitting on the edge of a beautiful bed with fluffy white pillows and soft blankets was Marianna. She looked wonderful. All sickness was gone. She looked more radiant than I ever remember her looking before. She had a peaceful smile on her face and a serenity about her that I have never seen.

She rose from the bed. We all embraced her. She said she had to be leaving now. She told us that she would always be near us. She told us that she loved us more than we would ever know. With that, she slowly disappeared and was gone. That was it. That was the end of my dream. When I awoke, I felt so much better. I knew Marianna was fine. I knew that she was with God, where there was no more pain or suffering. I sensed this to be true before this final dream, but now I knew it inexplicably as fact. I was not sure if this was my overactive imagination or a divine revelation from God. It did not matter. What did matter was how much better I felt.

When my father-in-law Giacomo, Marianna's husband, passed on, the only experience I had was a brief dream in which he told me, "I'm going to be with

Mom. . . . So long!" He was really happy. This is exactly how he lived his life, carefree and filled with joy. He departed quite effortlessly. We all missed him tremendously, but had comfort in knowing that he did not suffer endlessly the way his wife had, and that they were now together.

I have already shared with you the story of my unique experience in which my Grandpa Frazer came to visit me and massaged my feet. That was the most profound spiritual communication I have had the great pleasure of experiencing. It is so reassuring to have these gifts from beyond. It is truly a confirmation that life is everlasting, and that the bonds of love exist forevermore. Our loved ones have not died in spirit. The spirit, which is the most integral part of their true essence, lives on. If we wish to make a connection with that spirit, it is definitely possible. I hope to continue to make these contacts.

Recently I had a communication with a friend who has passed on. Glenn was only thirty-four years old when he died. His death was such a tragedy. He was not someone I was very close to in life, but I had known him for many, many years. One of our good friends, Andy, was Glenn's very best friend. Andy was so distraught over the death of his best buddy; I desperately wanted to be able to give him a message of healing. I asked God if I could please have a communication. The following is what I received.

Hey, Andrew, don't worry about me. I am fine. My dad met me at the light. It is wonderful to be here. I never told you but you are my best friend. I love you, man. I'll always be around; you will always be my best friend. Help my mom and little bro get through this. I feel really bad that I left them. It was just my time to go.

When you ride, think of me. I'll be sitting on your shoulders, cracking up. I didn't laugh enough in my life. Andrew, do lots of laughing. Enjoy all you've got. It goes by so fast. This place where I'm at is pretty okay. I was so tired. Tired of the whole thing. I just went to sleep and woke up in this great place. Keep going out, you need it. Don't be sad, I'm right here. I will send you a dream. We can still be friends in your dreams. We will ride all over hell and back in your dreams.

I know you won't ever forget me. We were like brothers, you and me. I will never forget you either. When it is your time I will be there to welcome you. You have a lot of living left, though. Enjoy it! Remember all the great times we had together! We went through a lot of shit! A lot of good shit!

Tell my mom I love her, please. I don't remember the last time I told her. It might have been when my father died. It is great to see my dad again. We are catching up on everything. Please help my mom. Please stay in touch with Georgie boy. He's gonna be fine, I know it. But it would make me feel better if I knew you were looking out for him. I miss you already. See you in your dreams!

Glenn

I gave this message to our friend Andy. He had not been able to fully grieve up until that point. As I spoke with him on the phone he cried. My friend Beth, Andy's wife, later told me he cried for hours. He was able to release a lot of the pain bottled up inside him. I can only hope that this will help him in his healing process.

God, I am really not sure if all these encounters have been through you, or are a mere figment of my imagination.

Was this my imagination or your divine intervention?

What difference does it make, my child? Your imagination is integral for creating your reality. You cannot accomplish any great thing without first imagining it. Imagination is the first step towards realization. God works in mysterious ways. One of these ways is through your imagination. Your highest thoughts, your grandest thoughts, are God's thoughts—one and the same. These highest thoughts will also be the clearest thoughts. They will be simple messages and they will contain truth. When you have a communication with a departed loved one, you will know it to be truth when the message is simple, positive, and loving. It brings a calm and peaceful serenity, which descends over your very being. The messages these loved ones bring to you are always similar. They are: "Do not worry," "Fear not," "I am happy," "All is well," "God is with me."

These messages will never be of fear or anything negative. If the message is truly coming from the spiritual realm, it will always be of love. If you wish to make contact with your loved ones, simply ask for the contact. It may be as subtle as a feeling or a vague sense of their presence. They will approach you only in ways that will not frighten you, which is the last thing they want to do. If you desire to have a true communication, it is totally possible you will.

The guidelines I have given to communicate with God are the very same guidelines to follow when you wish to communicate with anyone in the kingdom of Heaven. Be aware that you are in the presence of angels or spirits, whatever you wish to call them. They are with you always. They will make their presence known if you request it.

As you develop spiritually in an unselfish and noble manner, you will be able to draw these angels nearer to you. When you have one of these encounters, you will remember it always and your life will never be quite the same again. Enjoy these communications. Do not worry whether they are your imagination or my divinity. If they bring you joy, or love, or a sense of serenity, they are true. Angelic intervention sometimes goes beyond thought or feeling and becomes action. This is truly divine intervention. This is when an angel swoops down and protects you from harm's way. You have heard many stories about this type of intervention. A young child crosses a busy street with a car rapidly approaching, and as if by some miracle, the child escapes injury. Often this is the intervention of an angel.

Many of you have had brushes with death. Some of you have had numerous brushes. These close calls do not have to be as serious as nearly being run over by a car. Sometimes there are smaller interventions. For instance, you are walking on a beach, and hidden underneath the sand is a big, jagged piece of glass. You step right near it, but not on it. This is not even made known to your conscious mind. This was an angel gently preventing you from harming yourself. This is an intervention of which you were not even aware. Angels intervene in this way all the time.

There is an angel guiding every human being in his or her work. Sometimes an angel will help a doctor perform a medical miracle. Angels will often help the talented athlete accomplish the impossible. Angels will provide comfort to the dying and those they leave behind. Angels will lovingly guide you on a safe path while you are driving in your car. Do not become so angry when you miss your exit or get stuck in traffic. For all you know, it is an angel intervening for your benefit.

Angels are there to comfort you, protect you, guide you, warn you, and be a friend and companion when you are most lonely or afraid. Your loved ones' souls and angels are one and the same. Some angels have been watching over you your entire life. Others have joined in your guardianship after they passed from the physical world. Still other angels have been present in all your lives on Earth. There is a complicated hierarchy of these spirits. They all play different roles. They all possess important jobs. They all have their truest missions. And they are all of the light of God's love.

You have had several close calls when you know there were angels interceding for your welfare. Your readers might enjoy some of these very personal stories. I have given examples of this intervention, but not specific details. Tell of *your* experience, right now.

You want me to tell you of my experience with angels?

Yes.

I am not sure what is truly angelic and what is not.

Your heart speaks the truth, tell what is in your heart. I can think of at least three experiences you have had in the last several years that you consider angelic intervention. Tell of these experiences. This is your book, your story, and your truth. Tell of your *truth*.

God, I will always abide by your will, you have not asked anything of me. It is the least I can do.

The first story I remember happened when I was sixteen years old. I was out sailing on our sixteen-foot Hobie Cat with my boyfriend Giacomo (now my husband) and our two friends, Lisa and John. It was a sunny, mild day in October. There was not a single cloud in the sky. It appeared to be a perfect day for a sail. We were enjoying ourselves immensely, sailing on the Great South Bay. The wind seemed to be getting stronger and stronger. We were having a ball. We pulled in the mainsail, going faster and faster. In the distance we saw some dark, ominous clouds. The wind was getting gustier by the minute. We decided to tack one more time and then head back towards home. It was our last tack of the day. Giacomo was holding the line to the mainsail. I was holding the tiller, to steer the boat. We were moving really fast—flying like the wind. It was a great moment, when all of a sudden the boom snapped clean in half. We all went flying as the boat nearly flipped over. We were grateful we didn't end up "in the drink," but our little boat was incapacitated. We could not sail home without a sail. We thought that maybe if we tried to hold the boom together with one of our shirts, we could make it home. It didn't work. It was just too windy.

Now we were getting cold. We were drifting out farther and farther away from home. We were still joking around, but I was getting a little concerned. The sky was now black as night. I kept thinking that the mast surely would make a terrific lightning rod. The first crack of thunder was a wake-up call. We all looked at each other with the dismal thought that we really could be in danger. We were soaking wet, cold and shivering. We huddled together for warmth. That was when, excuse the expression, all hell broke loose. It started to pour. I mean, a downpour. Huge rain-drops pounded down on us. The wind came up. These were not just gusts. We were now in the midst of what is, around here, termed a "squall"—a brief, violent storm. The lightning flashed all around us. The thun-der was deafening. We were still drifting farther and farther from safety. We did not even have an oar on board. There was not a single boat in sight.

We were starting to really be afraid. I thought if Lisa did not start crying that I just might. The men were brave, but there was nothing they could do to get us out of our predicament. That was when I silently began to pray. I said to God, "Please send one of your angels." No sooner than I could count to five, we saw a boat approaching us. It drew near, and Giacomo tossed a man in a yellow rain slicker a line. We could not even see his face or hear his voice. Through hand signals we gestured what direction we wanted to be pulled in. We kept pointing to our creek, which is where home is. He pulled us all the way home. It took only about half an hour to be safely returned to our dock. I do not know to this day what kind of danger we were in. Was it mortal danger? I am not sure. I never had to find out, because God sent an angel.

There have been many times when I have prayed for God to help me. Sometimes it was for silly things such as finding my car keys when I was late for an important appointment. I never prayed until I was truly desperate. It is amazing, but whenever I did pray, I received the help I needed. I am forever grateful that God is so attentive to our prayers. There have been

other times when I did not even ask for help, yet I
believe that someone—be it angel, spirit, or God—
was definitely watching over me or one of the people
I love most dearly.

For my thirtieth birthday my husband gave me a wonderful gift. He painted our bedroom in a periwinkle blue and stenciled a border along the whole perimeter. Our daughter Marianna was toddling about. We had been working on the room for hours, trying to finish it before we went to bed for the night. We were fatigued. We were grouchy. We really should have quit, but we just wanted to get it done. My husband had an industrial-style light plugged in to fully illuminate the room. It was the only source of light. Earlier in the evening he warned me not to go near it because it was red-hot.

As we were finishing our work, Giacomo was on one side of the room and I was on the other. Marianna, the baby, walked into the room. She went over to the light. We both yelled, "Don't touch!" We sprang into action, running towards our child to prevent her from injuring herself. It seemed as if we were moving in slow motion. We did not get to her fast enough. She grabbed the light. Not just brushed it—grabbed it. Giacomo scooped her up and ran to the sink to run cold water over her hands. I waited for the scream. I felt sick to my stomach. The scream never came. In fact, Marianna was looking at us as if we were crazy. What is wrong with Mommy and Daddy? My husband put her down. We looked at her hands. There was no blister. They were not even the slightest bit red. "Boy," we thought, "how on Earth did she not get burned?" We were so happy that our precious child was just fine. She had a close call, but nothing had happened.

All of a sudden, I had the overwhelming feeling that something very special had just occurred. I really and truly felt that my mother-in-law Marianna, for whom our daughter is named, somehow had intervened and protected her from harm. I still believe in my heart that this is exactly what happened. I do not have any proof to speak of, I only know how I feel, and I simply feel that it was Marianna helping our little Marianna.

The most recent intervention occurred not too long ago. I was driving my daughter to speech therapy. She was securely belted in the backseat. We were running a little bit late. The speed limit was thirty-five miles per hour but I was driving well over the limit. I should not have been speeding. Unfortunately, we often do things that we should not be doing. That is why we need our angels all the more! Anyway, there were two lanes of traffic heading east and two lanes heading west. I was in the left-hand lane, moving eastbound. All of a sudden, in front of me I noticed a car coming from the opposite direction, trying to make a U-turn into my lane. I thought to myself, "Oh they're not going to go, they don't have enough time." Just as I drew nearer to the car, it pulled out in front of me! I had to move into the right-hand lane or hit it. My dilemma was that there was a car moving out from a side street turning into the right lane. Either way I was going to hit one of the cars.

In a split second I thought maybe I would jam on my brakes. I knew that I would not be able to stop! Somehow I jerked the wheel to the right, avoiding the car on my left, and then in a swift motion, I jerked the car to the left, avoiding the car coming out into the right lane. I have no idea whatsoever how I did this. I don't even know how my car fit through the space between these two cars. I felt like I had just experienced the weirdest type of "Twilight Zone" experience. As my daughter and I got through the two cars, I said aloud, "Thank you, God!" Anna said, "Mommy, what was that bump?" I told her I did not know, but I remembered that I had felt a bump too. My car had not a scratch on it. I had not hit either of the cars. It was weird, weird, *weird!* I told Anna how lucky we were.

I then went on to say that the angels must have helped us. She told me, "Mommy, I saw them." I was stunned. I asked her, "Marianna, what do you mean?" "The angels, Mommy, I saw them. They were pretty." I nearly fainted. The rest of the day I was shaken, not just from the near miss we had experienced but from my child's words. I do not know if she was making this up for my benefit. My daughter knows that I love angels. I could not help thinking that maybe she had seen something. We both certainly felt something. Nonetheless, we are truly blessed. God works in multitudes of mysterious ways. Do I believe in angels? You bet! Everyone should believe in them, you never know when one might be there to "bump" you along to safety!

I have been fortunate to have these experiences. I could tell many other stories that have happened to people I know. These would be second-hand stories if I told them. I do not want to do this. I invite anyone to tell me of their experiences of God's or angelic intervention on their behalf. My e-mail address and other pertinent information appear at the end of this book. Please send me your stories! I will try my best to reply to all who send them!

Once again God spoke to me in the form of poetry. These poetic verses are nearly as enlightening as the answers to my questions. Whenever God speaks to me, I feel compelled to write it down and share it with you.

The Dance

Revelation—
to make the unknown known
Divine Revelation—
to make the great unknown known

What is this great unknown?
the wondrous mysteries that set the universe in motion

constant motion, perpetual motion
vibrating, humming to the most glorious sound
the music of life
physical life, spiritual life

You are born into the physical, destined to die
and be reborn, once again into the spiritual
this is your rhythm—
one two three
one two three
life death rebirth
life death rebirth
It is a waltz
a wondrous waltz
the dance of eternity

Dance with *me* in *love*
be my partner
be passionate in your step
step lively and with purpose

Be quiet so you may feel the music
hear the melody
the music touches your soul

Some songs will inspire you to dream
some songs will inspire you to plan
some songs will inspire you to create
when we are partners in this dance
all songs will inspire you to love

Sing this song loud, sing it clear
you can listen as well as you hear
listen to the love within
It is the most vital, integral, beautiful part of you
It is what gives your soul life

Life death rebirth
one two three
one two three . . .

My family is such an integral part of my life. I am fortunate that we all live nearby one another. We have had many joyous holidays together. Often these holidays have revolved around of all things—food! We lovingly prepare meals for one another. One particular Easter my dad asked me to say the blessing. It happened to fall that year on March thirtieth, which is my son's birthday.

I was caught off guard by Dad's request. Elder family members usually say the blessing. When I spoke, I spoke from the heart to God, thanking him for our many gifts and blessings. I got really choked up. I honestly cannot even tell you what words came flowing from me. Nonetheless, everyone was moved by my blessing. My aunt came to me and said she really enjoyed my simple message from the heart. We then enjoyed a wonderful meal together.

Why is food a sacred experience to some people?

First let me say that every moment in your life is sacred. You recognize this sacredness often when you are grateful for the abundance in your lives. When friends and family gather together to eat at the same table, they take in spiritual nourishment as well as the nourishing food. It is as if they were eating at God's table. When grace is said before a meal, it elevates the experience to another level. You are all reminded of the great riches you possess. You are reminded that you eat to live, you do not live to eat. You gather together to celebrate the joy in the mutual sharing of your ideas, your common love for one another. Recognize in each other that your lives have great meaning.

It is not an accident that you are together in this life. Make the most of your choices. Your very existence has great purpose. Your actions make a difference in the world. Lift up the spirits of those you love and hold dearest in your heart. Tell them you love them; you need their love in your life. It is as essential as the wonderful meal you are about to partake.

Make time for giving this message of love to one another. Do not wait too long to show kindness, you may very well lose the opportunity. Your life is brief, the mere blink of an eye. Live each day to its fullest. This is a simple message often overlooked. Say grace on a regular basis, not just on holidays and special occasions. Rejoice in all that you have. You are blessed. You have a blessed family that loves you. You have loyal friends who love you. You have a God who loves you, eternally.

I have encountered this blessing over the years on several occasions. It is a message that many will relate to. It can be said at any occasion. A blessing for all reasons, all seasons. The author is unknown.

May the good Lord give you:
Enough happiness to keep you content
Enough trials to keep you strong
Enough sorrow to keep you human
Enough hope to keep you happy
Enough failure to keep you humble
Enough success to keep you eager
Enough friends to give you comfort
Enough wealth to meet your needs
Enough enthusiasm to look forward
Enough faith to banish depression
Enough determination to make each day better than yesterday,
And may we in turn thank you, oh God, for your blessings.

There are seven sacred wonders of the world. These have been chosen, above all else, by man as wonders.

What is the most sacred wonder of the world?

Oh yes, the seven wonders you speak of are splendid creations of God and man. There are many, many more wonders worthy of this "list." The wonders that God created—canyons so grand carved into the Earth, enchantingly beautiful waterfalls, immense redwood trees designed by God to live eternally. All this I created to awe and inspire, to move you to recognize your very soul. Do they speak to you in this manner? So many wonders—the great oceans abundant with life, the stony cold mountain that man is compelled to conquer, the rolling emerald green hills that give way to lush valleys where you picnic, the black sand beach where you dip your toes in the cooling turquoise water. The wonders of God are unlimited in number. God will always create new wonders to inspire and astound his children.

Through this inspiration man has created wonders that nearly rival God's creations: the great pyramids miraculously created by the diligent work of many men; the Great Wall of China, endless miles stretching across the huge country of China. On a clear day this wonder can even be seen from the moon! Oh, the ability mankind inherently possesses to create! It is wondrous in itself. Cathedrals, churches, mosques, and temples of worship, all beautifully created by man in the name of God. God looks down at his blessed children and God is awed and inspired! These creations of man, sacred and holy, only demonstrate further the tremendous power man possesses.

When a great number of people gather together with a common goal in mind, unbelievable wonders may be created, *are* created. Understand that you are all simply smaller pieces of the whole, which is God. You have the infinite power within to create, just as God creates. Anything that is created with love in the heart is sacred. The special meal you create for your family is sacred. The home, the refuge you build for yourself and those you love, is sacred. The garden you plant and the bountiful fruits of your labor are sacred.

Even the trivial is sacred when love is present—the loaf of bread you bake, the bouquet of flowers you carefully pick and present to the one you love, the photographs you take with your Olympus Super Zoom 2800. (*I think God is throwing this in to make me laugh.*) These photos are sacred because they have been taken with the eyes of love.

Even Disney World is sacred! How many people make a pilgrimage to this wondrous place and nearly have a "religious" experience. Walt Disney was a great humanitarian with love in his heart. His dream arose from this love. You all have the power to create your own Disney World! You do not need to have such lofty aspirations. I am only trying to demonstrate the great creative power within you. Enjoy the simple splendor of *your* creations.

When you gaze at your children sleeping sweetly, realize this is your greatest creation. This is your legacy to the world. Tend to your children. Value them as the wondrous creations they are. Realize that you are a wonder as well. Every child, every human being is truly wondrous. No two are alike. All are special and miraculous in their own way. In all the years of eternity there has never been an individual exactly as you are. You are unique.

You, my child, ask me, "God, what is the most sacred wonder?" The absolute most sacred wonder of the world, the most sacred wonder of the entire universe, is something that I have tried to explain through the writing of this book. I have tried to explain this great "thing" through my many prophets. The most wonderful books have been written about the essence of this thing. The most pleasing, exalted artwork from every far corner of the world, from every culture, in every century of man's existence has been created to demonstrate the beauty of this thing.

All manner of expression—language, dance, song—has been put into use to express the wondrous beauty of this thing. This wonder I am speaking of is God's greatest gift to the universe. It can never be destroyed. It can forever change form but it will forever endure. I am speaking of the *soul*. Within your soul lie three things: love, joy, and spirit. These three things are all one and the same. You may even use these words interchangeably.

Think about this. If you had a very best friend (now, this is your dream friend), someone who made you unbelievably happy whenever you were in their presence, this person would possess all the wonderful godly attributes of kindness, generosity, integrity—all things that are good. If such a person did exist, you would say, "Wow! This wonderful person I know, what zest they have for life, they truly have . . .

"Love.

"Joy.

"Spirit."

These three are all the *soul*. It is this *soul* that is the most sacred of all wonders.

God, I love summer. Please give me some inspirational words on the glory of today.

To you, my child, summer is sacred. Here are my words for you:

Summer

Just as the heat of the day becomes too much to bear,
just when you seek shelter from the glaring sun's rays,
the gentle caress of God's breath is upon your shoulder.
Cooling you with utmost tenderness.
The summer wind is sacred.
Fragrance of ripened flowers drifts upon the wind,
the sweet smell of summers past.

The carefree summers of children playing,
free from life's burdens.
Water sprites frolicking in the ocean, the pool, the sprinkler.
Be lighthearted; be like the child of your memory.
The memories are sacred.
Play on a hot summer day, refresh and gladden your spirit.
The waters are before you.
To be outdoors, the splendor of nature before you . . .
To dive into the cooling waters of summer
is to experience bliss.
The waters are sacred.
The opportunity for bliss is before you.
Do not let it pass you by.
The cold, stark winter will descend in due time.
But summer is *now*.
Now is the moment.
Enjoy simple moments.
Bask in the sacredness of summer.

Thank you so much, dear God. That is truly beautiful.

Show me your thanks by heeding these words. Enjoy!

Okay, God, This is a big one generally speaking for the whole of humanity:

What is the purpose of life?

This is the biggest question for all mankind. Ultimately, this is the "big" question I spoke of earlier in our writings. The answer is different for each individual. I notice you have asked the question in general terms. There truly are no general answers. But God will tell you that one key thing is the common purpose for *all*. This purpose is for God to be God, through you. For you to be you, through you. Understand that they are one and the same. You *are* God—lesser, smaller pieces of the whole, which is God. God already *knows* what God is. You already *know* what you are. Your soul eternally has all this knowledge within. Your common life purpose, the purpose of all mankind, is that you need to *experience* that which you already *know*.

Knowing something and experiencing something are two distinctly different things. You know that a ripened pineapple is sweetly tangy just by looking at it, just by holding it in your two hands. But when you get through the spiny exterior to the beautiful flesh inside, and break off a piece or slice into it and place it in your mouth, it is then that you *experience* this pineapple.

God (and your soul) choose to *experience* time and time again. You come from an eternal Heaven in which you *know* *all*. In this heavenly existence, there is nothing which you are not. You are the all-knowing essence.

God created your existence in the physical world for you to experience who you are. As you create in this physical world, you create who you are; you experience who you are. I realize this concept of *knowing* and *experiencing* is difficult for you to grasp. It is difficult for most to grasp. It really does not matter. You truly do not need to understand this. The question, "What is life's purpose?" is the question every single one of my children asks at some point in their lifetime. My point is, do not concern yourself with the answer. The mere fact that you ask the question, "What is *my* purpose?" *is your purpose!*

Your entire life is a series of revelations, which form the answer to this question. Your entire physical existence over many lifetimes is the progression towards this answer. This is the big question. The big answer requires eternity to answer. Unless, of course, you make the choice to simply *know* the answer and not *experience* it. You already know it—not in your conscious mind, or in your physical existence—but in your soul's existence, in God's kingdom. It is to Heaven that you will always return. If you choose to remain there, it is your choice. You certainly do exist in this place called Heaven, just as you exist in the here and now.

Your heavenly existence is quite a different thing from your present existence. It is glorious, wonderful beyond words. I cannot use words to explain or describe this existence. In due time you will know and understand. For now, *experience* all that makes you feel good, all that brings you joy, all that is *love*. You are on the path, dear child. This is the required first step in working towards answering the question you ask.

Through your life's path you will help many along the way. Others on a similar path will in turn help *you* along the way. This is a cooperative group effort. To truly answer the great mysteries of life, to truly bring them into your conscious mind, into your physical existence, all people must be on the path—the path towards all things good. You have forever to accomplish this. I will say to you once again, the joy is in the journey, not the journey's end!

That was a wonderful answer. I notice we keep going over some of the same things again and again.

Yes, that is right. We do keep going over the same subjects. We discuss different aspects each time. Look for new bits of information being provided here. It is necessary to go over these topics again and again. Do not be insulted, but collectively you are all a little dense. This is not your fault. God created you to have amnesia in this world. It is all part of remembering what your truest purpose is. You cannot remember that which you already know. So in this physical life you know nothing. You are innocent babies born with so much heavenly knowledge, but no earthly knowledge. You grow rapidly, learning and ever changing, constantly acquiring the Earth knowledge you need to survive and make a life for yourself. You have forgotten all the knowledge that you once possessed in Heaven.

There is a great void in your life that must be filled. Some of you fill this with compulsive behavior. Some fill it with material things. Some fill it with perversion and corruption. Some fill it with taking care of others. Some fill it with creating beautiful things. Some fill it with religion. How you fill this void will determine your level of satisfaction in this life. If you fill the void with something that is good, something that is positive, you will find happiness and satisfaction in your existence.

But it is not until you fill this void with *God* that you will truly be full. Filled up to the very top with *love*. Yes! My child, I will repeat myself again and again. The message I am bringing to you is not altogether different than others that I have brought. These messages again and again have the same underlying truths. The times will change, but truth does not change. I will forevermore speak to my children— guiding them towards their larger truth. Your soul and God are linked together forever. Whether you choose to recognize this or not is free-will choice.

Not all my children recognize my existence. I simply cannot get through to everyone. You will know these children I cannot get through to. These are the tortured souls that make the news headlines day in and day out. Your connection with the source of God's love enables you to endure anything that comes your way.

I am very sad for those who do not make the connection. They go through life with eyes that cannot see, ears that cannot hear. They are truly handicapped in all sense of the word. In death, upon their life review, they will recognize and understand what they missed in life, how much their lives could have been better. The lesson learned will be a painful one. Through this pain they can experience the pleasure of knowing God and then experiencing God in their next life. This does not happen for every soul. Realize you are lucky in this regard. Count this as one of your many blessings.

In some of your lifetimes you have not made this connection

as well. You have walked in many different shoes in many different lives. Ultimately you choose to know God. Ultimately you choose to experience God. This is your mission. It is everyone's larger mission. You all have smaller missions within this larger mission. These smaller missions play very important roles in the progress you are all making.

This great awakening cannot be accomplished unless many, many people unite to diligently work to accomplish the smaller tasks needed to get the end result. Eventually all people will unite. In this unity is strength. In this strength is power. In this power the greater good will be achieved. Yes, I am repeating myself with this message. It is a message that bears repeating.

> *When I was younger, I mostly spoke to you, God, when I needed your help or assistance. As I got older I spoke to you more and more on a daily basis. Basically I would pray for you to watch over all the people I loved. Or I would pray for silly, trivial things.*
>
> *Now I pray only about what is very important to me—things worthy of your attention. I do not want to bother God with silly things. God has enough to worry about. You used to be a "sometimes thing" in my life. Now you are an "always thing." I like this relationship. Since you began speaking to me I cannot tell you how happy I am.*
>
> *In the past I tried to find you through religion. I found that for myself, the way to find you was through me. I never even thought to look in such a place. I understand now that I am you. This is thinking pretty highly of myself. Some people may think I am extremely full of myself in thinking that I am God. If someone had told me this several months ago, I would have thought the same thing.*
>
> *How remarkable your communication has been. I have grown, changed, and progressed in so many ways. Thank you so much, dear God. Thank you*

from the bottom of my heart. I think I now know the true meaning of this life I am living. I have an understanding of what this meaning is. But I still do not think I am capable of living this understanding every day. I want to do this, I just don't quite know how.

Living this understanding—how can I do this?

You can live this understanding! Really *you can!* In simply knowing, in simply trying, you are nearly there. So many people do not even try. They have given up. Do not be so hard on yourself. You can achieve living this understanding at any given moment. You must simply choose to do it and not ever change your mind. If you become uneasy in your ability to do this, seek me out. Talk to me. Quiet yourself. I will always speak to you. I will never leave you. I am here whenever you need me. Sometimes when you need me, you forget that I am ever-present.

You say that you do not wish to pray for silly, trivial things. Pray, *pray!* Make the connection, silly or not. If you are giving it your attention, your time, your thought—it is not silly at all. Anything you take notice of, that eats up your energy, is worthy of hashing out with God. Do not be afraid of "bothering" me. I cannot be bothered.

God listens to every prayer. *You* have the hidden ability to answer every prayer. God cannot do this for you. God can provide the guidance so that you may find your own answers. But these answers are still coming from within. You did not know you had these answers, did you? You are of God. You *have* all the answers. Yes, people will say, "Who does she think she is?"

You yourself would have said these very words a short time ago. But that is in the past. This is *now*. The people who read this will come to this information because somehow they were looking for it. They may not even realize they were looking for it. Even as they are reading it, they may not realize this. But the information contained herein will haunt them. It will stay with them. They will think about it, even if it is just one small aspect. Something will spark their interest, and they will not be quite the same. That is why you are writing this. That is one of numerous reasons. These reasons will continue to unfold and become clear to you over time. This is a work in progress. Even when you think that you are "done," you will *never* be done.

You have much work to do with regard to our communication. Oh! The joy that awaits you! Keep talking to me. I will forever talk back. This dialogue is not going to end. You have already made that choice and there is no going back. You do not desire to go back. We may only go forward together. You will realize your life purpose in going forth together. Does it not make you happy to know this? I always know what is in your heart. You cannot hide from me. Do not think you can deceive God. Can you deceive yourself? Can you trick yourself? Of course not—*you know what is true.*

The meaning of *your* life is *your truth.* Individuals must seek to find their own truth, their own path. Living this understanding, living the understanding that is God, requires true dedication to do just that. I will never tell you it is easy. If it were easy, everyone would be doing it. In doing *it* you will be eternally filled with *love*, eternally filled with *joy*, and filled with your eternal *spirit*. Remember, these are all the essence of your *soul*. This is what *it* is all about! Not many have been able to achieve this. *This* is a very high aspiration indeed. You can do this if it is what you truly want. If you are not ready to make a complete and total commitment to live your life this way, every day—it is not a terrible waste or tragedy. Your life is precious. Your life is never, ever a waste. No one's life is a waste. This is not possible. Continue trying.

As I told your small children, Jake and Marianna, "Begin the next day fresh. It is a new day, a day that you can start all over. Any mistakes that are made the day before should be forgotten. Try to be good to one another on this new day."

This is good advice for little children. It is good advice for you. Heed these words. And always remember, as I told your little ones, "I love you, my dear little children."

About five months ago I began a creative frenzy that still has not ceased. I make my living as a graphic artist, so I am a creative being. This is my passion. This book, my latest creation, has been my biggest passion ever. When I work on it late at night I am not even the least bit tired.

Normally if I stayed up working half the night, I would be exhausted. I have noticed that whenever I am doing what I love, time does not seem to exist. I do not notice if minutes or hours have passed. It is only when my vision begins to blur that I realize it is time for rest.

I understand the passion and insanity that some artists, composers, and creative geniuses have experienced. It is in this insanity that the most beautiful things are created. Sometimes when I am in a creative frenzy, I truly feel that something greater than myself is working through me and merely using my body as an instrument for expression.

I once created an angel mosaic on my living room floor. For about a week I worked on it every night from about ten to two or three in the morning. In the daytime, I did not experience the creative process in the same ecstatic manner. I preferred to work at night. I became so absorbed in the task. It really turned out so beautifully. I love it! Everyone who enters my home notices it immediately. It is the hearth of my home. It is the spiritual center of our dwelling.

This angel I created floats between night and day, forever protecting our home with boundless love. God, I ask you, was there some force greater than myself who helped me to create this thing of beauty?

Do you help us in our creation?

My dear one, *you* are a creative genius! When you are "in sync" with the creative force of God, you experience these ecstatic moments of creation. This is a blessed occurrence. The feeling of something greater than yourself working through you is not untrue. There is some great force at work. This great force is your connection to the divine—the all-loving connection that you are making with the source of God. This just goes to show you how much can be accomplished when a connection is made. God is not responsible for your creativity. You are responsible. You are also responsible for making the connection with this unending, enormous love.

Your mosaic is truly beautiful. You take all the credit. You still would have created it, no matter what—this is *your* talent. Through our connection you not only created it, you *experienced it*. What a wonder it is to experience your very own creation. Your heart and your soul are a part of this creation. I mean that this is you—you are the angel. One of your grandest wishes is to create beauty. Day and night, create beauty in the world. Did you not know that when you created this angel, it was a self-portrait?

No, but you might be right about that!

Of course I am right. God is never wrong, silly. Now, do you realize what you are to do with it?

Please, please, by all means tell me!

It is your heavenly *spirit* spreading beauty, light, and love to the whole world below. It is perfection. It is perfection because it was created with pure love in your heart. This is the love you aspire to; this is the very love you would like to have present in your life at all times. This is a gentle, beautiful, inspiring reminder that love is always there. You simply need to find it. It is perfect to include on our book cover.

Oh God, thank you! You are so wise! You are of course right! I considered using this somehow, but I did not realize its perfection. I was not sure until you explained things to me.

Why did you create human beings?

Understand that you are all special. God created you to be unique, unlike any other beings. It is not possible to create a being that has the physical attributes of God. This is the unknown essence of which I speak. God is everything with regard to physical properties—God is a blade of grass, a bird flying overhead, the great blue whale, every beast of the field and forest, and God is *man*. God is *everything* that is *living* in the entire *universe*.

In the Bible it says, "God created man in his own image, in the image of God." These words speak the truth. In creating mankind, God gave the human *soul* all godly attributes. God gave his children the ability to have complete free will in the physical and mental capacities of human flesh. When a person dies, the soul is no longer encumbered by its physical existence. The soul always returns to God. This is where it came from and this is where it shall return.

In the kingdom of Heaven the soul knows exactly what and who it is. But it cannot *experience* this. This is a problem for God as well. God chooses to experience God through you. This is why all human beings were created. God created humans so that God could experience life in the physical world. Every one of God's children is but a piece of God. We have spoken of this time and time again. The soul of man knows no boundaries. It has the potential to be of God in the physical world as well as in the kingdom of Heaven. Animals are uniquely beautiful and have their own souls. But the soul of an animal can progress only so far. The animal soul has its limitations.

I created man with the innate ability for the soul to grow continuously with no limits. Originally, man's sole purpose was survival. This early man I speak of did not yet possess a human soul. This man had a soul like the soul of an animal. When reference to Adam is made in the Christian Bible (I speak of this because this is what you know), it is said, "And the Lord God formed man of dust of the ground, and breathed into his nostrils the breath of life; and man became a *living being*." This "living being" spoken of is the *new* man. This new man did not possess the soul of an animal with its limitations. This new man possessed the soul of God. The soul of God is *all* things, animal included.

Human beings have progressed significantly in their evolutionary process. They have evolved intellectually, physically, and spiritually as well. This spirituality is always present within. It is merely hidden and forgotten soon after birth into the physical world. As human beings, you forever search to "get in touch with" this part of your being. This is the most important part of your being. When people connect with soul, they may say, "I have found God!" They indeed have. They realize that God was always there, always present.

Let me provide you with a modern-day analogy on this. Your body is like a TV set. God is like the broadcasting station, beaming down a signal to the TV set. This signal transforms itself into somewhat of a miracle, which is your favorite program. If the television set is broken, you will not be able to see the program you wanted to watch. This does not mean that the signal is not coming from the station. Soul is ever-present; whether or not you recognize this is your own personal choice.

If you recognize the presence of your soul within, of God within, you will truly be blessed with infinite light, wisdom and love. Your joyous discovery of soul is all part of God's great plan. Some people claim to be "born again." These are people who have found soul. Whether you practice any particular religion does not matter. Whatever terminology you prefer to use, the end result is what's important: *recognition of soul.*

What is the fate of those who do not recognize God?

Remember, all my children *do* recognize God. Some simply do not realize this. If you believe in your own existence, you believe in God. Your free will enables you to make decisions regarding your spiritual beliefs. These beliefs are the reality you create for yourself. If an individual believes that God does not exist, this is because they have a preconceived idea of what God is.

God is *everything*. There is no way to not believe. Those who pass from the physical world into the world of soul, the kingdom of Heaven, soon find out the true essence of the great force, of God. This force is not at all what they expected. This force is not at all what *you* have expected. This force is something that cannot even be grasped slightly by your being. All my children return to me. This is the fate of believer and nonbeliever. This is the fate of *all.*

What do you have in mind for me today?

My wonderful child, what a concept! Do not struggle on this day. Nurture your soul today. Do not fight the process. Give in to the quiet time that you need for yourself. Make an effort to experience this time. It is in these quiet moments of reflection that genius is born. There is genius within. Today, trust that this is true. Rather than fighting to take control of everything, put your trust in God that everything will work out just fine. Your task in the physical world is not to be God. Your task is simply to be human and to recognize God, to recognize soul. Live your life with love in your heart. This is the simplest way to recognize soul. This will bring joy to your existence here on Earth.

Try to reduce the everyday stress in your life. This stress prohibits your connection with the divine. You know this. This has been a problem for you in the last few days. Do not worry, it shall pass. Let go and simply live. Living involves participation. Do not be a bystander. Do not spend so much time thinking about doing *it*. Instead, *just do it*.

It is soul-nourishing to be around people who have this attitude as well. People who simply *live* each day to its fullest. Do not spend too much time being around people who are not open-minded to the soul experience. It is simply too exhausting for you to be in the company of people who are not open to the idea of change. If you can help to motivate these people to seek change, so be it. With change there is growth. Do not be afraid of change. Change is necessary for progress to be made.

It is important for you as a member of the human race to learn new things on an ongoing basis. Surround yourself with people you find to be uplifting and fun. When you delight in the company of another and they feel the same about you, then your combined energies are astounding. This is positive energy flowing in the finest conceivable way.

Spend more of your time in nature; this is what God would like *you* to have in mind for yourself. When you participate fully in your life, you will be amazed at how good you will feel. This is your responsibility to yourself. You have many, many responsibilities to others. Do not forget yourself. Your responsibility to yourself is to find love in everything you encounter, to seek joy in everyday affairs, to spread this love and joy to others, and to *live your life* with full participation. Do not remain in the sidelines, get in the game!

My husband and I indulge in few luxuries, but one of our pleasures is membership at a small yacht club, which is just a few short blocks from our house. We consider it our vacation every summer. It is a great place for kids to grow up. Our children take swimming lessons every day and our son is learning to sail. Pretty exciting stuff! Anyway, on the Fourth of July they have sailing races all weekend. Other sailors from all over Long Island compete in the event. It is almost impossible to get within a block of the club. My kids and I packed supplies for the entire day—two coolers, two tote bags, life jackets, sweatshirts, and a twelve-foot-long crab net into the car. As we approached, parked cars lined each side of the street. There was not a single parking space. I asked my kids, "Should we try to find a spot inside, in the parking lot?"

Then I said, "If we say a prayer to the parking lot angels . . . maybe there will be a spot." So the three of us chanted, "Oh! Parking lot angels, please let there be a spot." We said this a few times. As we rounded the corner, there was a spot—right in front, basically VIP parking! We thanked the angels and had a terrific day. By now my kids are accustomed to their mom's wacky behavior. Hey, whatever works . . . Do not deny the power of "ask and you shall receive."

Well, the funny part is, one morning after this incident, I drove my kids to their daily swim lesson. Normally there's no problem parking. It is only insanely crowded when there are races. So on this particular morning, I pulled into the parking lot, found a place in front, and parked my car. I did not think at all about what I just had done. My daughter looked at me and said, "Mommy, you forgot to thank the parking lot angels!"

Many people limit what they believe in to the natural world. They acknowledge only what they can see or what can be explained scientifically. I always thought there were supernatural forces at work but I did not truly believe in these forces until I personally experienced them. I have been blessed to experience these mysterious forces that cannot be explained in any conventional manner. Every person has the right to believe whatever they wish. Through God's words I have learned that every person has their own truth. Individual truths vary. But universal truth cannot be denied. I personally believe that every living person has a responsibility to believe in universal truth. This truth, of course, is what I call "God." I think that it is not possible for mankind to really make progress until every person meets their responsibility—to make a connection with the divine, all-powerful, all-loving, creative source of God.

Do we have a responsibility to connect with God?

Yes, my precious child, you are correct. Every human being does have responsibility to connect with the all-powerful source of love, which is God. When I say "responsibility," I want you to break this word down into two separate words. They are "response" and "ability." Now switch the order of these two words. Every person has the *ability* to *respond*. Not all realize their ability. Respond means to answer, to have a reaction.

God calls to all his children. God speaks in ways too numerous to list. Do all children respond to my calling? No, they do not. But *all* have the *ability* to *respond*. Responsibility simply is finding your own way to make the connection with the source. It does not matter how you do this. God cannot stress this enough. The method by which you meet this responsibility does not matter.

You are right about man's progression. When the responsibility is met, and the connection with God has been made by each and every individual, a wondrous transformation will occur. This awakening will be unlike anything mankind has experienced before. At one point in time, people did not believe the world was round. There was no scientific proof. Those people had the right to believe the world was flat, but they had the responsibility to investigate further—to grow, to learn, to change their perception about things.

It would be foolish to accept something as truth merely because someone else tells you that it is true. You must search for your own truth. Respect the truth of others. You each need to know, and experience for yourselves, your individual truth. You all have the responsibility and the ability to respond to God. This is a *universal truth*. This is one of the universal truths all my children are seeking.

Many are lacking this truth I speak of. Many are searching for something. That something is the love of God. It is ever present. It is always waiting for your response, for your positive reaction. Know that you all have the ability to respond. You all have the *need* to respond. Your soul has the hidden desire to respond.

The task that you have as human beings is to bring what the soul desires into the conscious mind/being. If this is accomplished, you have met your "responsibility." This is not only your responsibility to God, it is your responsibility to your very self. It is your responsibility to the entire human race. This is *everyone's* responsibility.

Last night I took my kids for a quick bite to eat at a local fast-food place. I was in a bad mood. I was trying to overcome this. I thought to myself, "Why am I so miserable?" I looked to my left and there was a young woman with a little girl about six years old. I looked at her and thought she must be the little girl's big sister. We ended up sitting next to each other. I soon realized that she was the child's mother. We began a conversation. We talked for about fifteen minutes.

I found out that she had been just sixteen years old when she had her little girl. She was a single mom, struggling to raise her daughter alone. I asked if she had finished high school. She had gotten her degree through the mail. My kids got some silly toy with their meal. I overheard the little girl asking her mother for a toy. In a soft voice she told her, "Honey, we can't do it today." My son Jake wanted to get an ice cream. I gave him the money and he got on line. I got an idea to buy the little girl the toy she wanted. I hoped that this young mother would not be offended.

I joined my son in line, gave him more money, and told him what to do. He walked over and handed the toy to the little girl. The smile on her face was more than enough thanks to me. The young woman offered me the change in her purse. I told her that she had to accept kindness. People do not give kindness freely unless they truly want to. She smiled and said thank you.

We then continued to talk. I discovered that she was trying to get a job in an office. She had taken some courses and was now seeking employment. She told me she had just come from the office supply store next door and had faxed several résumés in reply to different want ads. With each résumé she sent a cover letter and a reference. I was impressed with her. I thought this girl deserved a chance. She complained that it was so expensive to send a fax—three dollars for the first page and two dollars for each page after. She told me she had four more resumés she wanted to send out. She had sent only three of them because she needed money to buy her daughter dinner. I told her, "I have a fax machine at home, if you give me your resume I will gladly send it for you." She looked at me with amazement. She asked, "Are you sure?" I told her, "Absolutely!" She gave me the three pages that needed to be sent. She thanked me.

She then went on to tell me that she had experienced a really rotten day. Then she said I was "like an angel sent to her." I found out her name is Amy. I took her resumé home and I promptly sent it for her. I truly hope she gets a job and that everything works out. I have her resumé on file just in case I know of anyone looking for a gal Friday. I felt I had made a friend from a complete stranger. This is a wonderful feeling.

God, I cannot tell you how much this young woman's exact words meant to me—her reference to me as an angel. They brought me more happiness than I could have ever brought to her. This is what I want to do. I want to be a living angel. This is what I aspire to. I want to make a difference in the lives of many. It could be a simple small kindness or it could be on a grand scale. This is how I want to spend my days. I do not want to typeset menus any longer. I do not mean that I want to entirely give up "working." But I only want to take on jobs that make me feel good about what I am doing. Is this possible, dear God? Can I not just aspire to be a living angel in people's lives?

Can I be a living angel?

What a wonderful aspiration! Why, of course, you can be anything you wish to be. You, my child, have discovered your calling. *You have discovered your purpose.* Congratulations! This is *your* big question. Now answer it. Go out and *be* a living angel. Go out and spread love and kindness to total strangers. Uplift those who seek it. And for those who do not, help them to see the light. Through this book we have written together, you will come into the lives of many people. Some will be touched profoundly by these very words. Some will say that this book is a blessing and it has changed their life.

Do you see how many people can be helped through you? Do you realize the implications of this? You are humble in your beliefs. Your modesty is quite charming. But understand, there will be people affected in a positive way by this.

This is what you want. This is the grandest desire of your being—to help, to guide, to uplift, and to bring the message of God to many. This message is *love.*

You have already begun some work to do this. You will be doing much, *much* more! In a year's time you will realize just what I am getting at. You have a grand purpose. I will not reveal that to you right now. This is something that must be slowly revealed to you. This is something that you are slowly creating.

There are many small, baby steps to get where you are going. You have much work to do. This work I speak of will bring you more happiness and satisfaction than the work you are currently doing. You need to slowly make the transition from the living you made for the last ten years of your life. You should not give it up "cold turkey." You will always do some of this type of work. Your creativity is an integral part of you. This creativity will help you reach your ultimate goals. These goals await you. You do not even know yet what these goals are. I promise you this, my child: your life will be blessed. You will not be free of struggle. That is part of your earthly existence. Struggles are necessary. Struggles are what make success so sweet. You *will* make a difference. This is your desire.

> *Oh dear God! Is this possible? Of course it is. Your words tell me that it is so. I trust in you God, completely. My faith is steadfast. Thank you, dear God! I am so happy to hear this news from you. I feel that I can achieve whatever I set out to do. The reason I can do this is that I am working toward the greater good. I am spreading love. How can I live up to this? God, as you know, I am far from perfect, I am far from being a saint.*

Can I live up to your expectations of me?

I have no expectations. Have you not been listening to me all along? These are your expectations. These are your aspirations. Trust in *yourself*, have faith in *you*. You can make this a reality; this is your desire. Now *just do it*. Don't worry if you are not a saint; whoever said that all angels are saints? You are an angel because you keep trying. Your vision quest is one that is so positive, so powerful, so transforming to all who encounter *you*. Just keep working at this vision of yours—that picture inside your head of how you want things to be. This picture is your focus. This is creative visualization. If you can visualize something, if you can create it in your mind, you are able to then create it in your reality. This is true for everyone.

Gentle readers, know that *all* this is possible for you as well. Find your own vision quest. *All* things are possible with *love* in your hearts. You too can speak with me. Use this book as a guide, as an inspiration to speak with me. My child, Yvonne, is but an example of this possibility. It is necessary for me to speak to many. It is necessary so that this great awakening I speak of may be set in motion. You may choose not to hear my voice. This is okay. There are many reasons for this. Whether or not we have a mutual communication, I will get through to you, if you desire it.

If you are looking for divine guidance, you will receive it. God's methods of communication are not merely with words. If you seek a communication, watch for it. It will come to you in a manner that is comfortable to you. Do not fear. God is always *all-loving*. God will not come to you in ways that frighten you. When religion speaks of God in a way that portrays the Essence with great force and fury, this is simply not a true picture.

The fury inflicted is from the great masses of people, not from God. God does not seek revenge on his children. How could this possibly be an all-loving God? I have explained that the combined energies of the great masses, the collective consciousness of a large group, have extreme negative and/or positive repercussions. The catastrophic effects are staggering. The combined power of the great masses is astounding.

This is not God. God is there to help you pick up the pieces after a tragedy. God is there to inspire, to guide, to uplift, and love when you need God the most in your life.

There are people who believe God has struck them down like a bolt of lightning for their sins. These people have begged for God's mercy and have profoundly changed their ways for the better, for the greater good. This is of their own creation. This is what they needed to make the change.

God provided them with the ability to create this for themselves, but God is not the bolt of lightning, striking them down. Remember that your power within is not something you are conscious of. You are aware of only a very small percentage of this power. As man progresses he will be able to tap into more and more of this source of power. As long as the power is used for the greater good, more and more will be made available. You have no limitations, even in this physical world.

You have the power to create Heaven on Earth. This is not an easy task. This is a task that may not be realized for a very, very long time. This is the result I speak of. You all have a long way to go before you get to this ultimate end. This goal is inevitable. Just as the sun shall rise. In time, the sun shall rise over a new world, a new universe. The old will have passed away. The new will be very different from what you know in this present existence.

The wonders that await you—this is why your soul keeps on coming back. Your soul knows what wonders await. Your soul wishes to be an active participant. Your soul does not merely want to know what the future holds. Your soul desires to experience what the future holds. Most of you choose to have this experience. Those who do not remain in a place that I cannot even begin to help you to grasp. This kingdom of Heaven, which is the term you use, is so wondrous. If you choose to remain here forevermore, that is not at all a bad thing. That is a wonderful thing.

There is much work to be done in Heaven as well. Very different work than the work you are accustomed to, but work nonetheless. Whether you are in the heavenly realm of existence or the physical, earthly realm, you have work to do. You are constantly *becoming* that which you *are*. I do not want to get into this too much. My aim is not to confuse you. But you are constantly at work. Effort must be made to slowly and with difficulty become all that you can be.

In human form, a specific state of being is necessary if you are to realize your full soul potential. You are constantly progressing towards this full soul potential. There is progress to be made, no matter what form you are in. The human condition and the soul condition are always progressing toward complete godliness. In being mere pieces of the greater puzzle, which is God, you seek to unite and complete the whole puzzle. This is your *ultimate* potential.

I think I now know what to do. I do not know the exact steps I must take, but I completely trust that I will find out. I am not worried about it. It is wonderful to not worry about it. I have spent so many years of my life filled with worry. It is a tremendous relief to not have this burden any longer. I really wish I could help others to let their worries and fears go as well. Trust that with love in your heart, your greater purpose will be revealed to you. Your life's work will have meaning. Despite your struggles, you will be blessed.

Now you are getting *"it."* I have gotten through. We have made great progress. We are nearly done.

What do you mean by this? I am not ready to be done!

Nearly done. We have a few more things to discuss. But all good things must soon come to an end. Do not look at this as an end, but as a new beginning. One door closes and another opens. There are new doors out there for you to knock on. Keep writing. Keep speaking with me. You do not always have to write down everything that is said. I will answer questions anytime you ask them. You will know which answers need to be written down. You will know which answers are for *all*.

We have much to do together. The work I speak of is an ongoing, forever thing. When I say we are nearly done, I merely mean we are nearly done with this first leg of our journey together. It is a long journey. You said at the very beginning of this book, on your Acknowledgments page, "I would like to express my gratitude to all those who have helped me on my own spiritual path. It has been a long journey and I still have far to go." You wrote this at the very beginning of our experience together. You had written only a dozen or so pages, yet you were so perceptive in making this statement. Yes, you do have far to go on your journey. The journey is far from over. Delight in this journey. Enjoy this journey for what it is, for what it has the potential to *be*.

God, your words never cease to amaze me. I look forward to the next leg of this journey. I am in joyful anticipation of the things that are yet to be. I realize that you have been ever-present in my life's journey, in my soul's journey. I cannot help remembering the poem Footprints. This particular poem brought to light the meaning of God's love for so many people all over the world. It is a simple message, filled with tenderness. It is also a powerful message portraying an image of God carrying us through troubled times.

Footprints

One night a man had a dream . . . He dreamed he was walking along the beach with the Lord. Across the sky flashed scenes from his life. For each scene he noticed two sets of footprints in the sand—one belonging to him, and the other to the Lord.

When the last scene of his life flashed before him, he looked back at the footprints in the sand. He noticed that many times along the path of his life there was only one set of footprints. He also noticed that it happened at the very lowest and saddest times in his life.

This really bothered him, and he questioned the Lord about it: "Lord, you said that once I decided to follow you, you'd walk with me all the way. But I have noticed that during the most troublesome times in my life, there is only one set of footprints. I don't understand why when I needed you most, you would leave me."

The Lord God whispered, "My son, my precious child, I love you and I would never leave you. During the times of trial and suffering, when you see only one set of footprints, it was then that I carried you."

Margaret Fishback-Powers

I find these words so comforting. To know that God is ever-present in our lives is a wonderful realization. These words spoke to me the very minute I read them. I think they would speak to most people. Now when I read this poem, it has even greater meaning to me. I will be forever altered by the communication I have had with God. I will not look at anything in quite the same manner as I did before. What has occurred for me is truly amazing. Once again, thank you, dear God, for allowing this to happen for me.

You are very welcome. It is my greatest pleasure to bring these words to you, to bring these words to others, through you. I want you to take a break my child. I want you to come back to me in three days' time. You need time to reflect on what we have written together. I want you to reread all the pages and then sit with them for these few days.

Dear God, I am sorry. I know you said to take a break, but I don't want to wait the three days. I need to communicate with you now. I have something on my mind.

Oh, my child, patience is not one of your virtues. It is not necessary to ask for my forgiveness, this you already have. Now, tell me what is on your mind.

My daughter, Marianna, has been sick for the last few days. She probably has some sort of virus. Her only symptoms are a fever and she's been very grouchy and needs to sleep a lot more than usual. The night before she got the fever, I was up with her from about one to three in the morning. She had terrible cramps in her legs. It was the first time this ever happened to her. When I was her age, I experienced the same thing. My mother called them growing pains. Marianna was in agony. It is terrible how much these cramps can hurt. The last time I had them was when I was pregnant with her.

My poor baby was shrieking in pain. The muscles were in a spasm. I felt so bad. I tried to help her by massaging her legs, distracting her by singing to her, and stroking her hair. Nothing was working to calm her down. Once in a while her screams would ease to crying. She cried for nearly two hours. It was terrible.

The worst thing in the world for me is to see my children suffer. I looked into her eyes. She was not herself at all, but I connected with those big green eyes. Her eyes were saying, "Help me, Mommy." I was beginning to get exhausted. I just didn't know what I could do to help her. It is often in my desperation that I pray to God for assistance. In a loud voice, inside my head, I said, "Dear God, please help me to take this pain away. Send your powerful, loving energy through me."

I felt a loving energy fill me. It can be described as a feeling of warmth that filled my body. It went down both my arms and passed into my hands and then into my fingertips. I placed my hands over her legs. I did not actually touch them. I moved my hands slowly over her legs. I felt almost a magnetic attraction between her legs and my hands. I don't know how else to explain it.

I felt as if my hands were being pulled towards her legs and pushed away from her legs all at the same time. In the space between my hands and her legs, I felt a warm sort of glow. I could not see it, but I could feel it. I have no idea if this was something I dreamed up out of my strong desire to help my little one to ease her pain. But before I could count to five her crying stopped. She immediately fell into a deep sleep.

Can I possibly have the power to heal?

Your prayer, my precious one, your prayer was simply heard by me. Your request for healing was made earnestly from your heart. You *did* help your daughter's pain to simply vanish. When I say "help," I use this word because your little one, your beloved Marianna, also helped. She was simply ready to let the pain go. You can provide healing to those you send God's love-energy. Those who receive this healing must be receptive to it. You cannot miraculously heal those who do not desire to be healed. Some choose to be in pain. Still others choose to be in sickness. Your daughter did not choose to have her pain. But she did choose to swim in the pool all day long. Her little legs were simply tired. Her choice had its natural, physical consequences.

Often, physical pain or sickness arise out of the choices you make as human beings encumbered by the physical body. If you choose to smoke two packs of cigarettes a day for twenty years, there is a good chance there will be consequences to deal with. I am not telling you that all sickness or injury is created because of your actions. Often these decisions are made by the soul before even entering the physical body. Hence the expression of wisdom, "It was just her time."

The warmth you felt, the energy field, was that of pure love. God's pure love. This connection with the great, all-powerful, all-loving source of God has unbelievable power for healing. It is possible to channel this love I speak of in many, many ways. It can provide inspiration, healing, hope for things better, and knowledge.

The connection with this love has no boundaries. It can be used for the greater good in any conceivable manner. You simply tapped into it the very same way that you tapped into it to write this book. You will not be able to channel this love/power for healing unless there is really a desperate need from your heart/soul to do this. It is just like when you were stranded on that boat when you were a girl of sixteen. It was not until you were truly, desperately frightened that you prayed for God's intervention. It was then that you received it.

Do not pray for healing of things that are trivial to you. It will not work. You will know these things are trivial. You cannot

deceive yourself. If you think about the times in which you desperately and earnestly prayed to God with a loving heart, your
prayers were always realized. It can be brought into the conscious experience. God provides the tools for you to do this.
But know and understand that *you do it.*

When you pray desperately and earnestly for another, it
is possible for you to help them, but they may have their own
agenda. The healer has the intention of channeling love and
healing—the recipient needs to believe, desire, and accept
this healing. If their soul does not want your help, you cannot help them. If their physical mind/body does not want
your help you cannot help them either. There must be an
acceptance of healing or it cannot occur. But if there is an
intention to heal and an acceptance or belief in the healing,
then miracles can take place.

These miracles happen every day. For example, a woman
is stricken with cancer. She has massive, deadly tumors growing in her body. She is sent home to die. This woman is not
ready. She has much living left to do. She has not finished
the work she anticipated to accomplish. Her will is strong.
She has connected with her soul and her soul has chosen to
remain. She has complete faith in her God. She has many
loved ones desperate for her care, desperate for her survival.
Together they earnestly pray.

Several weeks later the woman feels a little bit tired but
absolutely marvelous. She is convinced that the cancer has left
her. She calls her doctor. The doctor is doubtful but intrigued
by the joy and the energy in this dear woman's voice. He tells
her to come in that very afternoon, he had a cancellation. The
medical team does several tests. The doctor personally redoes
the tests. He is speechless. The cancer is evidently gone.
There is no sign whatsoever that the disease was ever present. The great power of love is astounding. *These miracles
happen every day!*

Now, my child, with that to reflect upon, I would like you
to take a break of at least a day or two. Please do not think

about any questions you have right now. Think about all the pages you have written. Reflect upon them. Digest their meaning. You need to do this.

Hi God! I'm back.

Oh, my dear child, what a surprise!

Is that sarcasm, God?

Yes. What are your questions, my precious child?

Thank you, God, for being so understanding. There are some conflicts in our writing. My grandmother, Doris, brought one to my attention, and she has a valid point.

My impatient one, if you had given yourself more time to ponder what we had written together, you may have realized this on your own. I know the inconsistencies you speak of. We do need to clarify a few details. Remember, God is always looking out for your best interest. Trust that this is so. When that voice tells you to wait, *wait*. Be patient. You have a very hard time doing this. You have infinite patience with others. With your husband, your small children, your many loved ones.

But you have no patience with yourself. When you want something, you want it instantly. The value of patience is a lesson you must learn. Now, regarding these conflicts you speak of, what is on your mind?

Well, in the beginning of the book you say, "You on this Earth are all pieces of God. Beautiful, wonderful pieces encompassing every characterization of what God can be. Good, evil—everything there is." Then later it is said that God is all things good. I believe this is said several times. How can God be good and evil and then be all things good as well?

This is a very difficult aspect of my essence to explain. It is a paradox of sorts. It seems contradictory, but it is true, in fact. God is, indeed, *all* things. Within all things there is good and evil. The entire physical universe operates on the basis of opposite polarities. There is the up and the down, the in and the out, the big and the small, the here and the there, the finite and the infinite.

In experiencing *physical life*, you *know* nothing. In order to know, you must experience. In order to experience good and know what is good, you must also experience evil, to be able to know and understand the difference. This is essential to your physical existence, which is an existence based on experience.

Your whole purpose for existing in this world is that you may come to know what you already knew in the heavenly realm. God created his children for the sole purpose of God being able to experience what God knows. God is *you*, God is *me*. The many souls who walk the Earth are drops of water in an endless sea, which is God.

The whole, which is God, is infinitely larger and more complex than the smaller soul pieces. Certainly not all of God's children encumbered by the earthly body of flesh are all things that are good. If there is a "devil," the physical realm is where the devil lives. The only hell there is, is the hell you choose to create on Earth. This is part of your earthly condition. This is part of *life*. This is simply what makes you human, mere mortal beings.

To know something as fact, to bring it into your conscious mind, you must first experience it. The evil that exists in the physical world is just as necessary as the good, which exists. For you to understand and bring into your conscious mind all godly attributes that are good—to experience this goodness you must also experience things that are characterized as not good. You cannot know sweet until you know bitter.

Man's progression is towards all things that are good. This is where you will ultimately end up. This is your final destination. God is indeed everything that is good. This speaks the truth of the *heavenly* realm. When it is said that God is all things that are good, this is God in my truest form. This is God in my most perfect form. This is the all-knowing God of Heaven.

Your souls and the force of God exist in a state of utter perfection in this heavenly realm. Within this perfection there is only good. You know of that which is good. There is no evil to speak of in this place. The God of Earth, the God of experience is *you*. It is all my blessed children of the physical world, the world of experience.

God is *all* things. God is all things within both the physical and the spiritual realm. The kingdom of Heaven is wondrous in that it is all things that are good. There is no possibility for evil. It simply does not exist. There is no need for it. This place called Heaven is love in its absolute, pure form. When love is pure, there is only good. So yes, my child, God *is all things*—good, evil, everything. It all depends on whether you are speaking of the all-knowing God of Heaven or the physical God of experience. It is difficult for you to grasp that you are all God.

We are all part of an energy form that is connected, that is one. The dimensions of the physical world and the spiritual world are very different indeed. You are not children of a lesser God, a God that is good and evil within the limitations of physical existence. There is a greater God of spirit. You are all children of this greater God. Within this are *all things that are good*.

> *That has made it much clearer. Thank you! I am worried, dear God. I am worried that I will have more questions. Will I ever feel that this book is complete?*

You will always have more to ask of me. Do not worry. Do not despair. This is going to be one door closing. Many, many other new doors will open for you. You have many discoveries ahead. You will always have more to ask of me. There are so many questions still remaining to be answered.

Understand that this is an ongoing project we will be working on. The ending of this book only means that you can bring the beautiful messages of love to many others. This is the whole purpose of these writings. This is a huge part of *your purpose*. There is still much to be revealed. At some point you must end our first volume together. There will be others to follow.

The point in time is drawing near. There are people out there waiting for your message, God's message. The time is upon us. The time is now. Be patient, dear one, do not make haste. The awakening has begun. My children are waking from a long slumber. They are ready, they are eager for renewal of spirit. They are ready to remember that which inherently they have always known in spirit form. Be of service to these dear souls searching for answers. Assist them in bringing God's words to them. Encourage those with open minds and hearts to seek their own truth. This book was written for all those who are searching for their own answers.

Dear God, I don't believe I will ever feel as if I am truly done with this book. I understand that there will be more to come. This brings me great comfort. I have had sufficient time to reflect upon our writings. I have gained so much insight, such wondrous knowledge. The greatest comfort is knowing that there is so much more to come after this life. Through our death, there is rebirth.

My loved ones who have passed on are simply in the heavenly dimension. They still have a presence in my life, and if I wish to make contact with them it is definitely possible to do this. It is within everyone's power to do this.

It has also been a comfort to know that our physical existence has a purpose, that somehow our earthly existence, so fragile and such a quick, fleeting moment, is preparing all of us for something greater and more wonderful than we can ever grasp or understand. And we may return to this incredible earthly existence if it is our desire.

We can return again and again to experience physical life, gaining knowledge and constantly evolving towards the greater good of all mankind, constantly moving closer to an existence based on a state of pure love. This is what everyone's truest potential is. This pure love is the universal truth. This truth is the one truth.

Individual beliefs are all true as well. Every religious tradition is unique and beautiful and it is the truth for the individual believer. But beneath all these individual truths, the underlying common denominator is the universal truth of love. Mankind cannot make any real progress until the reality of these truths is recognized.

We are now in the midst of a great spiritual awakening. Slowly, slowly humanity is opening its eyes to a new spiritual awareness. This awareness is not a religion, although religion can play a part in it. This awareness is found within your very soul and the connection you make with the all-knowing, all-powerful, all-loving, God.

We are all God—little tiny pieces, but God nonetheless. This is truly a big discovery for me. A discovery I never thought about or realized before this book was written. There are many answered questions that have proved to surprise me, even astound me. Many of the questions were asked because I just did not know the answers. I was desperately seeking truth. These truths are my truth, but they will speak to many.

The journey of the soul is an ongoing journey. It is a journey that will last for all of eternity. There is no end. There is a mysterious connection of all things—people, animals, the beauty of nature, the Earth, the stars, and the universe—all pieces of the whole, which is God. If you are able to harness this pure love of the divine, then little by little your soul will progress. You will be able to uplift others as well and help them to progress too.

If you live with love in your heart on a day-to-day basis, miracles can occur. Our connection with soul is crucial—crucial to our ability to feel a sense of gratitude and wonder at our lives and the lives of others. Through this connection we act in kindness towards others.

When you can feel and appreciate the love of God and make the connection with this love, your whole world, your whole existence, begins to change in a very positive way. If all people make an effort to live this way, then great healing may be accomplished.

By raising our awareness, by connecting with God, filling our hearts, our souls, our minds, our being with this love, we then are able to heal ourselves, then our loved ones, then our neighbors, then our communities, then our towns, cities, states, countries, continents, the entire world! Together we can set this transformation in motion, together we can change the world!

Bravo! Very good, my child. You have been listening. It pleases me very much. I think you may be ready to conquer the world. Keep connecting with the love. Anything, *everything* is possible when you are able to maintain the connection of this love-energy. It will keep filling you up. There is an endless supply. "Your cup runneth over." When you spread this love to others, the love you send forth will immediately be replaced by the source. The great bounty of this love will increase all the more.

The more you give, the more you receive in return. It is a beautiful ebb and flow of love everlasting. Like the tides, love cannot stand still. It is perpetual. It is forevermore. This love is *the* great mysterious force, an infinite living energy, the all-powerful, the creator, the supreme being, the light, the truth, the infinite spirit, the almighty Lord, *God*. My dear children, one and *all*, know and understand that this love, this God, is the *great universal truth*.

In the journeys of your lives, you will discover this universal truth. You will embrace this universal truth as your own. You are but a part of the whole, which is this truth. Your purpose is the discovery of this truth. This truth is part of your soul's memory, forgotten by your earthly condition. You are to remember. This is so that you can *experience* this universal love/truth.

You will find that there is a process to be discovered to reach your true potential. This process works through each and every one of God's children. This process is utter perfection. There are no mistakes. There is simply change and growth and moving toward the greater good of *all*. As each and every one discovers this universal truth, in the journey of your lives you will find all that is needed is found within. You create your reality. The combined energy of many creates a worldwide reality—a universal reality. All of humanity is connected. All living things are connected. All energy forms are connected. The substance that links all things together is love. If you break everything down to its simplest form, its simplest structure, you are left with love. This is the essence of all things.

Trust in the process of your life unfolding. Trust in this all-powerful love. There is a great spiritual awakening in progress all around you. This awakening will have its obstacles. There will be difficulties along the way. All things that have worth, that have glory within, require suffering as well. The higher truth, the universal love/truth I speak of, will emerge. It is inevitable. It is the destiny of all. When a newborn babe tumbles out into the world, the child must take its first breath. It must learn to walk before it can run. It will stumble and fall. It will ultimately triumph. This baby does not question the process of its growth, its change.

Do not question your process. Trust in it. You will find that when a connection has been made with divine love—call it what you wish: God, Lord, Jesus, Father, Mother, Jehovah, Yahweh, the Almighty, Goddess, the Holy Spirit, Allah, Brahma, Buddha, the Creator, the Supreme Being—the winding path you take will lead you to exactly where you want to go.

You will find happiness when you stop seeking it. You will exist peacefully in the world. You will find joy in all things. You will find beauty in all things. You will be blessed eternally when you trust in universal love. You will open yourself to the great wisdom of this love. You will become one with the great power of this love. Ultimately you will reach your greatest, grandest potential of pure godly love. This is your destiny. This is everyone's destiny.

Destiny

Inevitable,
predetermined,
where you are going to end up,
how you are going to *be*—
your ultimate goal and purpose.

But—so much more. Oh! So much more.

The destiny of love is the
most glorious, enchantingly beautiful,
joyful, passionate, tender, gentle, kind,
radiant, magnificent, powerful—light.

Come, my children
unto the light, return to me.
Do not fear. God's true glory awaits you . . .
Perfection.

Rejoice in your earthly existence . . .
In your life, you unknowingly possess this perfection.
This perfection is ever-present. It must be revealed.
Discover your true destiny in *this* life.

You know perfection in Heaven,
you experience this perfection on Earth.
Turn those fleeting moments of love into love everlasting.
For this is your *truest* destiny.
This is the destiny of love.

Thank you for those beautiful words! Thank you for my many gifts and blessings.

Dear God, you have given me so much through the writing of this book. The effects have been staggering. My truest desire from my heart is that many will benefit from this. I have no idea what is in store for me. But I remain completely confident that it will be for the greater good of all. My faith in this is enormous. I know that the path I need to take will suddenly, as if by magic, appear at my feet. This does not mean that there will not be rocks to trip over or occasional detours. I realize this. Ultimately thy will be done. My will be done, on Earth as it is in Heaven.

My destiny is unfolding. It is day by day revealing itself to me. The knowledge I have gained herein is not the end. It is a fresh new beginning. It is like the light at the end of a long and winding tunnel. Beyond the tunnel is a whole new bright world of discovery. It is never too late to be what we have the true potential of becoming.

I can sum up this entire book by saying, "Live a life of love, pure love. Do it. Live it. Be it. The greater good of all will follow."

Please, join me on this journey. We are all in this together. With this newfound awareness, we will seek change. It is my highest hope that this book will bring you closer to this pure love that God speaks of so eloquently. This is everyone's truest mission. That is all there is.

In Closing

I can't believe I wrote the whole thing! Thank you so much for joining me on my extraordinary journey of spirit. Please remember for yourself that my journey is my truth, my reality. Seek your own truth. Create your own reality. You are never alone in your journey. God is always with you.

Awaken your spirit to the divine, and you will never feel loneliness or despair again. That is my wish for you. That is my wish for all. In experiencing my own personal awakening, I have reached a turning point in my life and I will never be the same again. I feel as if I have been given a chance to journey through life differently.

The effects of these writings will forever remain with me. It is the legacy that I will leave my children and the generations to follow. I truly feel that it is our children who are going to save this world of ours. I can look into my children's eyes and see the hope of a bright future. We must all work together to create a world that is worthy of its children. These children have been entrusted to us and are our greatest contribution to eternity. I ask you, "What does the future hold?" We have a choice. With love in our hearts anything is possible.

Special thanks to . . .

Barbara DiCioccio for graciously copyediting my manuscript with gentleness.

Debra Leslie for her beautiful Foreword and her loving guidance.

My parents, Bonnie and Pete, who have helped me on my path more than they will ever know.

My dear friend Tina for telling me, "You are an angel and I have always known this . . . now the world will know it too."

My sisters Andrea and Nicole and baby brother Petey. I love you more than I can tell.

My grandparents Doris and Pete. You are treasures that I thank God for every day.

My extreme gratitude to Hampton Roads Publishing for giving *Answers* the proper forum to be heard. Bob Friedman, you are a special man. You gave me not one chance, but two.

I would also like to thank Pat Adler, my editor at Hampton Roads. Pat, you are an absolute pro and a pleasure to work with. I hope we get the opportunity to work together again.

Many, many thanks to all who offered encouragement to me.

There are many I have not mentioned but I have not forgotten.

Love and gratitude to all,
Yvonne

Thank you, dear God, for my many gifts and blessings.

Index

About the Author

Yvonne M. Albanese lives on the south shore of Long Island with her husband and two children. This is her first book. She hopes to continue writing on the subject of spirituality and personal growth. Not knowing where the path will lead to, but trusting in a force greater than all of us that the right path will be the chosen one, she continues on her extraordinary journey of spirit. Hoping to always maintain the "divine connection," hoping to always receive the "answers" provided.

Yvonne Albanese would love to hear from you. If you have a story to tell, please share it with her. Your comments are valuable to her as well. She will try her very best to reply to all inquiries.

YAlbanese@aol.com

Hampton Roads Publishing Company

. . . for the evolving human spirit

Hampton Roads Publishing Company
publishes books on a variety of subjects including
metaphysics, health, complementary medicine,
visionary fiction, and other related topics.

For a copy of our latest catalog,
call toll-free, 800-766-8009,
or send your name and address to:

Hampton Roads Publishing Company, Inc.
1125 Stoney Ridge Road
Charlottesville, VA 22902
e-mail: hrpc@hrpub.com
www.hrpub.com